THE SPIRIT ALMANAC

THE SPIRIT ALMANAC

A MODERN GUIDE TO ANCIENT SELF-CARE

Emma Loewe and Lindsay Kellner

A TarcherPerigee Book

tarcherperigee

An imprint of Penguin Random House LLC
375 Hudson Street
New York, New York 10014

All illustrations © Charlotte Edey

TarcherPerigee with tp colophon is a registered trademark
of Penguin Random House LLC.

Most TarcherPerigee books are available at special quantity discounts for bulk
purchase for sales promotions, premiums, fund-raising, and educational needs. Special
books or book excerpts also can be created to fit specific needs. For details, write:
SpecialMarkets@penguinrandomhouse.com.

Library of Congress Cataloging-in-Publication Data
Names: Loewe, Emma, author. | Kellner, Lindsay, author.
Title: The spirit almanac : a modern guide to ancient
self-care / Emma Loewe, Lindsay Kellner.
Description: New York : TarcherPerigee, 2018. | Includes
bibliographical references and index. |
Identifiers: LCCN 2018020504 (print) | LCCN 2018027214 (ebook) |
ISBN 9780525504641 (ebook) | ISBN 9780143132714 (hardback)
Subjects: LCSH: Self-actualization (Psychology) | Mind and body. | BISAC:
BODY, MIND & SPIRIT / Reference. | BODY, MIND & SPIRIT / Inspiration &
Personal Growth. | BODY, MIND & SPIRIT / Healing / General.
Classification: LCC BF637.S4 (ebook) | LCC BF637.S4 L6396 2018 (print) |
DDC 158.1—dc23
LC record available at https://lccn.loc.gov/2018020504

Printed in the United States of America
1   3   5   7   9   10   8   6   4   2

BOOK DESIGN BY KATY RIEGEL

This book belongs to

....

Thank you,
Mom and Dad, for making
the whole world possible.
—EL

TO DAD,
You sparked my interest in the great beyond so many years
ago and I'm endlessly grateful for it. You'll always be my
spirit in the sky, and I miss you every day.

TO MOM,
Thank you a thousand times for your kindness toward and
service of others, myself included, and the gentle
but necessary reminder to slow down.
—LA(M)K

CONTENTS

PREFACE

OUR INTEREST IN RITUAL work stems from an innate curiosity about the personal practices that drive people.

As wellness editors, we're constantly in dialogue with MDs, herbalists, yoga teachers, athletes, chefs, and nearly everyone in between for their perspectives on what it means to live well and be truly healthy. Their insights are inevitably varied, shaped by their unique experiences and expertise. But we've noticed that they all somehow touch on the idea that physical well-being starts in the depths of the mind. It rises from the knowledge of who you are as a person, where your passions lie, and what makes you feel most yourself. Only by asking these big questions can we map out the specific, material steps that will bring us closer to our best lives. As we've listened to how people find their own way, personal ritual almost always plays an integral role.

Some rituals feel like massive undertakings; others, smaller commitments. Some are rooted in science; others, in faith. They can look like a staunch meditation schedule or an unwavering writing practice. A bath every evening or a solo walk in the mornings. A yoga flow or a running routine. While these may just seem like normal, run-of-the-mill habits, over

time they can become ingrained and imperative to those practicing them. They've gone from hobbies that entertain us to commitments that sustain us. They've turned into moments to press pause and observe the mind. Ultimately, they're what we turn to when it feels as if nothing else is left.

For this book, we gathered some of the most potent and powerful personal rituals we've ever come across, and we were even inspired to write some of our own. We have written these rituals into a calendar that's accessible to anyone. Along the way, we realized two big things: The history of rituals is just as important as their modern-day applications, and nobody knows how to explain a certain ritual better than those who do it every day. So, in the following pages, we'll trace rituals back to their fascinating beginnings and call on some of the foremost experts in the field to share how to carry them into today.

While many of our rituals are esoteric by nature, we root them in reality and ground them in science as often as we can, since we see equal value in reason, logic, and simple belief. In a world that is increasingly chaotic, disconnected, and sometimes downright scary, we hope that these rituals provide you with a sense of comfort. In the year that follows, use this book to tune out the noise and come back to yourself. It's in carving these little moments of stillness that those big, life-defining discoveries can be made.

Whether or not you have set rituals you've developed over time, we hope that *The Spirit Almanac* serves as a source of ideas and inspiration. By the end, you will be equipped with a selection of rituals to help you handle whatever life throws your way with ease, grace, integrity, and spirit.

Introduction

She was the type to fall in love with the moon, and
everything that was beautifully unreachable.

—Santi D.P.

The Spirit

SPIRIT: From the Latin word *spiritus*, meaning "breath, spirit," derived
from the Latin root *spirare*, which translates to "breathe."

THE WORD "SPIRIT" IS CHARGED WITH POLARITY. On the one hand, its definition has historically divided people time and again. And yet as much as religious philosophies vary in character, plot, and symbolism, the essence of spirit is remarkably similar across differing texts, traditions, and dogmas. Linguistically, the Latin root of the word "spirit" harkens to our breath—the life-force that animates us and unites us all in the human experience. In this definition, spirit is unifying. The breath is the thread that connects our higher selves to our physical bodies and to the common ground among us all. The spirit is our guide that helps us align with our heavenly truths and earthly purpose. Like breath, it is something we all share.

Our mission is to offer tools that create, nourish, and strengthen a connection with your own spirit through ritual. Not to be confused with ghosts of those passed, the spirit in *The Spirit Almanac* refers to the interaction of our souls—something we believe exists in each and every person—with powerful, larger-than-life forces cast upon us by the cosmos, the rhythms of nature, and ancient traditions that have been etched deeply into the surface of the earth through generations of ritual.

With a belief in spirit comes an element of surrender to magic, the divine, the universe, or whatever name you ascribe to the higher powers that be. But let's be real: We can't expect magic to do the work for us! A crucial component of magic is self-awareness informed by our ability to reflect, change, and grow. That's why we take an 80/20 approach. Eighty percent of our lives is the result of the vocational work we do here. The remaining 20 percent is magic: being in the right place at the right time, making that happenstance connection, saying yes when you want to say no.

Whatever influences us to make the decisions that change our lives is a product of spirit. The mystery of spirit is in our ability to direct it, call upon it, and trust it. Whether you believe in fate or the power of manifestation, we've all experienced those "coincidences" that simply seem as if they were meant to be. That is spirit at work.

While fitness and yoga have risen and fallen as wellness trends, the wave of interest in spirit is just beginning to crest. People are looking for comfort, answers, and changes that go beyond the scope of their own intellect and physical form.

Now more than ever, we are a society plagued by addictions of all kinds, a lack of purpose, indecision, and much more. Implementing a spiritual practice by carving out a structure to spend time with yourself is beneficial for you and everyone around you. It's only in commitment to personal growth that we learn what it means to feel connected with ourselves in the present moment. From that sacred space, we can forge meaningful relationships with one another and our life's work.

When everything is stripped away, spirit is what remains. Calling on yourself and your spirit through ritual is one of the most accessible, practical, and tangible ways to change your life.

THE RITUAL

Spiritual rituals are actions we repeat to feel and fuel our spirits. Rituals first came to us by way of religion, with roots in the Latin word *ritus*—a religious observance or ceremony. Communion in Christianity, bar and bat mitzvahs in Judaism—these are rituals we are all at least fleetingly familiar with. The secular rituals explored in this book, though, are a different kind of sacred.

They are deeply personal practices, separated from our routine by intention. Eating breakfast, for example, is a routine. But saying a pre-meal mantra and eating in silence with the intention of starting your morning in a slow, mindful way? That's the basis of a ritual. Your commute to work is a routine. Yet it too can be ritualized if you consistently use it as a time to remind yourself of three things for which you are grateful.

The ritualization of the mundane invites the mind to settle into the body. It creates opportunities to get quiet, to feel honestly, to look inward in a world that is begging us to look elsewhere. Over time, it can help us connect to spirit and share it with those around us. In turn, rituals are acts of self-care made radical in their ability to someday help others, as well as ourselves.

Ritual work is not a new concept. It stems from a rich history, shaped by our ancestors and passed down through lineages. Every culture from the beginning of time has carried through rituals to honor gods, the earth, and themselves. To be alive is to conduct such work.

Over the years, though, tales of ancient ritual have been relegated to books in dusty libraries. Recovering them from the page and applying them to the now can help us connect with generations come and gone.

By asking questions about why we're conducting our rituals and who did them before us, we're unlocking their true potential. We're embracing the present by way of the past.

And we don't need to do so alone. The renewed popularity of moon circles, sound baths, and other forms of spiritual gathering speak to our innate desire to look within ourselves, together. Inviting friends and loved ones into our rituals fuels bonds and forges connections. It also reminds us why we're doing the work in the first place.

This book will delve into the historic, social, and cultural significance of spiritual ritual work and will touch on some of the science that drives it along the way. We hope that this mix of science and faith, past and present, will appeal to everyone—no matter where on the spiritual spectrum they may fall.

THE SEASONS THROUGH HISTORY

The four seasons were our earliest timekeepers. Before the advent of TVs and laptops, the rhythms of the sun and moon were what informed and entertained us. Our ancestors let the natural world call the shots, plotting their harvests, ceremonies, and myths around its changes. They celebrated Mother Earth's four faces as reminders of the cyclical nature of time and space. And, though they really had no choice, those before us lived in unison with the outdoors. Getting outside was a way to feel informed and fulfilled.

Much has changed over the centuries, but the seasons that surround us—and many of the activities we do within them—have remained the same. In this way, seasons connect us to generations past.

Though perhaps not quite as much as our ancestors, we too find comfort in their predictability. After every spring comes summer, after every summer a fall and winter. In a modern world that's marked by instability, this consistency can be a relief.

But we think the seasons can be used as so much more than timekeepers. By letting the seasons inform our rituals, we are living *with* the earth, not just *within* it. By allowing the outer world to shape our inner work, we're reminding ourselves of the larger forces that are at play all around us and coming one step closer to transcending surface-level worry to achieve real, true, rich happiness. And isn't that what it's all about?

THE SEASONS TODAY

It's easy to get lost in the smaller cycles of existence—the alarm clock that sounds each morning, the daily grind, the commute to and from work. But when we let these habitual actions define our lives, we lose sight of everything that falls in between. Nature's cycle through the seasons, on the other hand, does not lend itself to monotony. The earth tilts and turns toward the sun in a glorious rotation that manifests as warmer and cooler temperatures, brighter and duller colors, crisp air and cool rain. It's a cycle unparalleled in its scope and drama. It's a show that reminds us of the universal forces at play, of the fact that time is at once fixed and finite and fleeting.

There are many ways to live in closer communion with nature's seasons. First, we can use them as checkpoints. Each one's arrival can be an opportunity to reevaluate how we are navigating life and a reminder that we need to continually check in with ourselves if we want to make real progress. The seasons can also serve as balancing forces. Each one carries a completely different energy, but they all need to play out before the year can come to a close. We can take a cue from them by relishing their polarities and embracing periods of introversion and extroversion, work and play.

Last, our reactions to seasons can shed light on our identity. Winter, with its short, frigid days and long nights, is a lonely and isolating season for some. Others might experience it as a soulful, introspective time to grow quieter and look within. Summer's harsh sun can leave some of us hot and irritable, but others find comfort in its intensity. Though the show we are all watching is the same, the way it affects us varies dramatically. How we immortalize each season in our minds provides clues about our personal needs and desires. We can learn a lot about our internal landscape by paying attention to how we react to our outer one.

This book uses spiritual rituals as tools to help us fully feel every season. Together, we'll recharge in winter, come alive in spring, shine in summer, and exhale in fall.

How to Use This Book

It is our hope that this book will bring you on a spiritual journey that takes its cues from tradition and the rhythms of the earth. You'll use the calendar's seasons and holidays—religious, astrological, and otherwise—as opportunities for pointed ritual work. While not an exhaustive list, the occasions you'll encounter all have great potential for growth and exploration. All in all, there will be eight to ten holidays called out per season, with a corresponding ritual tailored to the specific theme of each.

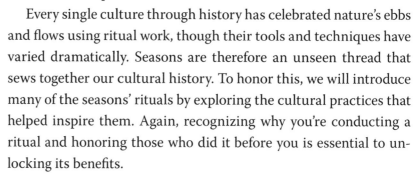

Every single culture through history has celebrated nature's ebbs and flows using ritual work, though their tools and techniques have varied dramatically. Seasons are therefore an unseen thread that sews together our cultural history. To honor this, we will introduce many of the seasons' rituals by exploring the cultural practices that helped inspire them. Again, recognizing why you're conducting a ritual and honoring those who did it before you is essential to unlocking its benefits.

The rituals themselves are designed by us unless otherwise stated, and we've worked to make them as approachable, easy, and enjoyable as possible. We know you're busy, so we made a point to shy away from anything that is too time or resource intensive. We recommend trying out each ritual on the day it is prescribed, or as close to it as possible, but it's no big deal if life gets in the way and you're running a few days late.

There are no hard-and-fast rules about where or when during the day to conduct your ritual, but it's probably a good idea to make rituals an electronic-free zone. Reserving moments and places to put down your phone and simply take care of yourself is powerful, and infusing your precious alone time with ritual and a little magical thinking can make for a seriously transformative habit. Beyond that, our only recommendation is to have fun with it, and don't complete any rituals you don't feel comfortable with. (Skip over our bendy yoga flow if you have a bad back, for example.)

Although we associate specific rituals with certain days, we know that rituals are not meant to be confined in such a way forever. Sometimes at the height of social summer, your body craves a little bit of winter's introspection. In the depths of fall's chill, we often seek out some of spring's freshness and levity. That's why at the end of every ritual, we'll provide ideas on how to translate it to the other 364 days of the year. While not every ritual will vibe with you (and that's totally okay), we hope you keep your favorite ones around, calling on them through each and every season moving forward. Practicing and personalizing them over days, weeks, months, and years will strengthen them. And even if you go on to repeat a single ritual every day, you will probably have a different experience each time. That's part of the fun: The journey to find yourself and discover your spirit is lifelong, and new insights will come with consistency, intention, and the changes of season.

A word about pronouns—in this text, we default to the feminine, but it's certainly not meant to be exclusive. Anyone, no matter their gender, can participate in these rituals and tap into the divine feminine within himself, herself, or themselves.

Get to Know the Terms

Before we dive in, let's run through the terms and ideas that fuel our rituals. Many of these words hold different meanings depending on who you ask. This is how we think of them and how they will be presented in this book:

* **DOWNLOADS**: When somebody says they "got a download," they mean an idea came to them, seemingly from out of nowhere. These insights feel more resonant than the random thoughts that pop into our heads throughout the day, and they speak to a higher consciousness or an inner knowing. For instance, you can have a download that a negative pattern you keep falling into stems from a specific moment in your childhood. Quieting the mind through ritual can free up space for these downloads to come through.

* EGO: Sigmund Freud coined the term "ego" to define the quick decisions we make from our rational brains. In psychology, the ego is therefore the surface part of our personalities that has been shaped by the world around us. If we live too much in our egos, we fall out of touch with our spirits—who we are before society told us who to be. As spiritual teacher Marianne Williamson put it, "Ego says, 'Once everything falls into place, I'll feel peace.' Spirit says, 'Find your peace, and everything will fall into place.'" The ego is the part of you that wants to keep pushing to get that promotion at all costs, while the spirit asks you to slow down and consider why you want it in the first place. We're all about stopping the ego in its tracks and nudging spirit to take its place.

* ENERGY: In a scientific sense, everything is energy. It is in a spirit sense too. The energy we refer to in this book is a force of magic. It's how you know someone is coming up behind you without turning around, and it's how you can instinctively feel what the person sitting next to you is thinking. Energy is a tangible force. Positive energy arises in those moments when light, sound, and feeling conspire to create some kind of electricity in the air. Likewise, you can feel negative energy as soon as you walk into a roomful of people who are stressed out. Becoming more attuned to the energy of everything is another benefit of conducting rituals that ask you to *feel* instead of *think*.

* GRATITUDE: Living with more gratitude is a proven way to be happier and healthier. By carving out time to remember a few of the things you are grateful for—be it on your morning commute or during your nightly meditation—you can actually change the way your brain processes the world. Maintaining a sense of gratitude (especially during difficult times when it doesn't feel as if there's a ton to be grateful for) is one of the cheapest, easiest ways to change your mood. We'll ask you to do so often.

* HOLD SPACE: To hold space for someone means to be there for them without judgment. This is especially important during communal rituals that involve a group share. Holding space for another person

means letting them know you are there to listen to their story without interfering or projecting. It means not offering them advice unless prompted and never making them feel shame or guilt for speaking their truth.

* **INTENTION**: Intention is the driving force behind every ritual in this book. Living with intention means asking "Why?" more and "How?" less. Assigning simple intentions to everyday tasks (e.g., setting an intention to journal as a means of self-discovery or to meditate as a way to de-stress) can help you become more attuned to what you really want out of life so you can then go chase it. It can also take the pressure off executing something perfectly—the why almost always matters more.

* **INTUITION**: While intuition is often ascribed to psychics and fortune-tellers, we are all intuitive beings. Intuition comes through as a feeling in the stomach, and it doesn't always match what's going on in the mind. It's pretty telling that the belly—the part of the body where intuition lives—is often the first place we restrict and suck in when we're self-conscious or scared. Living in tune with your intuition means following your hunches and trusting your gut, even when it's uncomfortable. The deep-belly breathing we'll walk you through in these rituals is meant to open you up to this magical power you inherently possess.

* **MAGIC**: It doesn't need to be as showy as pulling a rabbit out of a hat or making a coin disappear. Magic is anything that defies logic. The subtle (and sometimes not-so-subtle) feeling that the universe is trying to send you a message? That's magic in its truest, most elemental form. Through this book, we'll work to track down the magical in the everyday.

* **MANIFEST**: Manifesting your future is a way to wield some of your own magic. The word "abracadabra"—a notorious catchphrase of mystics—is Hebrew for "I create as I speak," and this is the perfect illustration of the term. True magic begins when you speak your truth and send a message to the universe that you're ready to change. Man-

ifesting means bringing a goal into being simply by speaking it aloud. You can manifest a new relationship or better finances, more confidence or less stress. The power comes in getting clear on what exactly it is that you want so that you can take actions that bring it to life.

* SPIRITUALITY: The phrases "spiritual journey" and "spiritual path" connote some sort of epic quest to uncover the deeper meaning of life. We see spirituality a little differently. It's not a means of discovering something new but a way of connecting with something ancient. Spiritual beings look to cut through the noise of modern-day life to get back to the simple truths that our ancestors celebrated: the allure of nature, the power of faith, and the fleetingness of time.

* VISUALIZE: Visualization and manifestation go hand in hand. If you want to call something into being, visualizing what it will look like in the context of your life is a powerful place to start. Visualizing your future is also a way to think about what you really want. We will often pull in visualizations at the beginning of our rituals to help identify what we're trying to get out of them.

* WITCHCRAFT: Hundreds of thousands of women (and some men too) were persecuted in the witch hunts of years past, simply for living out their truths. Today, a resurgence of witchcraft has taken magical thinking from a source of shame to an expression of feminism and power. As society begins to recognize women more and more, witchy undertones will only become more normalized. Though we will not discuss witchcraft specifically much in this book (mostly because it's such a rich topic that we can't do it justice in just a few pages), we see it as the underpinning of all these rituals. Ritual work is a type of witchcraft in that it creates something from nothing and uses elements from nature to build something magical.

THE SPIRIT ALMANAC

Introducing
YOUR SPIRIT TOOLKIT

N OW, LET'S RUN THROUGH the tools you'll experiment with during your rituals. We'll look at their power and purpose, dive into their history, and share how to get comfortable using them.

CRYSTALS

Crystals capture our attention with their sparkle and glimmer. Brought to us by way of occult shops and spiritual ceremony, the colorful stones have recently entered mainstream consciousness in a big way. Nowadays, it seems that mystics and skeptics alike are signing on to the stones. You can find them in dimly lit rooms that smell of sage and sandalwood and on display at local bookstores and beauty shops.

Part of their appeal is aesthetic. Crystals are pretty; plain and simple. They come in a rainbow of surprising hues: bright, vibrant oranges and deep purples that catch light in just the right way. The stones also come in many shapes and sizes to serve every need: Pocket-size ones feel like little portable charms, while larger ones can anchor our homes as grand, stately centerpieces. When placed next to one another, they offer a beautiful glimpse into Mama Earth and her many faces.

For many, though, the allure of crystals extends beyond the material. Since crystals are literal remnants of the earth, they are thought to hold the wisdom of millions of years within them. Simply interacting with the stones could cause some of this to rub off on us. Though there isn't much science backing up the efficacy of crystal cures, there is something undoubtedly medicinal about the idea that you can hold this little piece of the world in your hand.

For us, the power of crystals lies in how you relate to them. It's all about letting your crystals remind you of a certain intention. For example, let's say you pick up a green jade stone—one thought to help attract wealth and abundance—during a period of tight finances. The day you get your hands on the crystal, you think about what kind of financial abundance you're after and a few ways you can actively work toward it. Then, you place it on your desk so that every time you're sitting at your computer, you remember this goal. The stone then becomes a constant reminder of your desire to make more money, a little cheerleader holding you true to your intention. When you're approached with this perspective, it isn't so absurd to think that the crystal's presence can help you land a new job or get that raise you've been after. It comes back to the 80/20 approach. Change comes when you do the work, and a splash of enchanted earthly energy can only help.

THE STORY OF CRYSTALS

Our ancestors across cultures used these little pieces of the earth for healing of all sorts. The Egyptians buried their dead with a quartz to protect their journey to the afterlife; those in India used amber as a medicinal tool to bring balance back into the body; and ancient Greeks described the stones as a "sure [remedy] against every earthly woe" in an etching that dates back more than 1,500 years.

Various tales throughout the ages have imparted each crystal with its own unique personality. "Amethyst" comes from the Greek word for "not drunken," and wearing an amethyst necklace used to be a popular way to prevent drunkenness and hangovers. Greeks would rub crushed hematite

CRYSTALS

turquoise

citrine

quartz

carnelian

aventurine

amethyst

emerald

rose quartz

on their bodies before battle as a shield, and the stone is still thought to have a protective energy about it. Bright, vibrant citrine took on the reputation as a stone of good luck, rose quartz a promoter of love, turquoise a regal healer. Let's go over a few crystals and what they're typically used for today:

AMETHYST: Promotes spiritual growth and enhances intuition

AVENTURINE: Welcomes material wealth and emotional prosperity

CARNELIAN: Overcomes blocks and makes way for creative inspiration

CITRINE: Brings happiness, joy, and peace

EMERALD: Signals love and lasting success

TURQUOISE: Symbolizes protection, strength, and health

QUARTZ: Clear quartz brings clarity and power; rose quartz evokes love

FINDING THE RIGHT ONE FOR YOU

Crystals form when minerals join together and solidify into uniform, crystalline patterns. Different minerals fuse together under different temperatures, pressures, and conditions, which is why they come in such unique shapes and sizes. While some compositions (think clear quartz and amethyst) are common enough in nature to appear in pretty much every crystal shop, others are lauded rarities. Crystal collectors are willing to shell out millions for certain unusual stones, with a large blue cap tourmaline recently selling for $2.5 million and small chunks of meteorites going for $5,000 each.

Keeping this in mind, the first step of crystal shopping is nailing down a budget, but don't fret—many small-size crystals are inexpensive. Beyond that, you can visit a New Age shop, crystal store, or gem show without much of an agenda or preconceived idea of what sort of stone you want. As with most spiritual tools, if a crystal jumps out at you right away, chances are it's the one you're meant to have. From a more metaphysical perspective, you may need more of the energy it carries in your life right now, whether you realize it or not. This is also a way to explain why you may be pulled toward one crystal one month and another the next—it's all about your subconscious needs and desires. This is a reminder not to take a crystal's inherent properties too literally. No matter what a stone has been used for through time, it can always be exactly what you need it to be in the moment.

If you're struggling to find your crystal based on looks alone, make your search more tactile. Pick up a stone, hold it in your hands, and see if it evokes anything out of the ordinary. It may bring an image to mind, cause you to see a certain color, or literally give off a vibration in your palm.

Once you find one you feel drawn to, make sure it's actually from nature and not a lab. Phony stones tend to have air bubbles, be uniform in color, and have very deep cracks. They also reveal a white underbelly when you rub them a lot.

Since crystals are thought to pick up the energies, thoughts, and fingerprints of anyone who crosses their path, you should first metaphorically clean off your purchase before you welcome it into its new environment—be it your bedside, windowsill, altar, or desk. To do so, you can use a sage stick (more on those later) to bathe it in smoke, the moon to bathe it in light, or water, for a more literal bath. No matter how you choose to clean your crystal, the act of doing so is a sign that you're willing to welcome it into your life. Think of it like pressing its reset button, so it's attuned to you and you alone. Again, it's all about intention. You're asserting your possession over the crystal and expressing a willingness to work in communion with the tool.

From there, you can decide what exactly you want your new crystal to represent, what you want to use it to bring into your life right now. Strength? Love? Ease? The possibilities are endless.

HOW TO USE CRYSTALS

* **HOLD THEM WHILE MEDITATING**: Once you program your crystal with a specific intention, you can hold it in your hand during a meditation or visualization and picture bringing that intention to life.

* **WORK THEM INTO YOUR ALTAR**: Adding crystals to your altar (p. 41) is a really beautiful way to infuse the sacred space with an earthly, grounding energy.

* **GIVE THEM AS GIFTS**: Crystals make for unique, personal gifts. Choose a stone with inherent properties you think a friend or loved one could use. Be sure to cleanse it too, imparting it with your own stamp of positivity before passing it on.

* **CARRY THEM AROUND WITH YOU**: Small crystals can travel in your purse, pocket, or even bra as constant reminders of your connection to spirit and the earth.

RAPID—FIRE RITUALS

Here are a few of our favorite crystal rituals that can be completed in five minutes or less. Give them a try so you can become comfortable with the tool before diving into more involved seasonal rituals.

A CRYSTAL RITUAL TO CALM DOWN BEFORE BED

1. As you're lying down right before bed, place a small crystal on your forehead, between your eyebrows. This area corresponds to your third-eye chakra—thought to control our intuition and higher consciousness, according to ancient Indian tradition.
2. Close your eyes, take a few deep breaths, and picture the crystal pulling up any thoughts of worry or negativity lingering from the day. Envision freeing up space in your mind for dreams before placing your crystal on your nightstand for the next night.

You can also place a crystal on your chest before bed, and we've found that watching it rise and fall with our breath is really soothing.

A CRYSTAL RITUAL TO CLEANSE YOUR HOME

1. Fill a mason jar or bowl with water and place your crystal of choice within it to sit for a few hours or overnight.
2. Transfer the water to a spray bottle, adding a few drops of essential oil if you want a smell-good element.
3. Every time you feel down, stuck, or generally blah at home, take a minute to spray some of the crystal-infused water around to impart the air with your intention.

We like to make a new brew at the start of every season, choosing our crystal infusion based on what we could use more of at that time of year.

HERBS AND PLANTS

Herbs and plants are potent prescriptions, and they've served as medicines for eons. In fact, in certain native languages, the term for plants loosely translates to "those who take care of us." This bodes well for the plant-based diets we know so intimately from our work in the wellness world, but it also speaks to using plants in much smaller doses.

Herbalism, the ancient practice of utilizing herbs for physical and mental healing, is veiled in mystery and superstition. Early cultures associated herbs with an unseen spirit world, and the community members who spoke a plant's language were highly revered. Known as shamans and medicine men, these healers harnessed potent plant medicine in their quest to serve as conduits to higher realms.

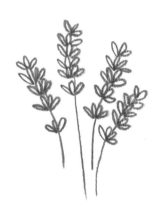

With the advent of modern medicine, we learned that the soothing properties of herbs can be isolated, extracted, and used to inform Western medicines. Even in today's age of synthetic drugs, most pharmaceuticals in America have been originally inspired by botanicals.

We've used science to explain so much of plant medicine that there's little room left to explore. However, some people are still eager to tap into the more enchanted and mysterious side of herbalism. Plant medicine ceremonies that administer potent brews like ayahuasca are popular among a cohort curious about spiritual journeys. People are flocking to the remote jungles of Costa Rica, or sometimes to the basements of Brooklyn, to be led into an unpredictable unknown.

THE STORY OF HERBS

The first written record detailing how to use herbs for health dates back an incredible five thousand years. A Chinese text called the *Shennong Ben Cao Jing*, loosely translated to *The Classic of Herbal Medicine*, introduces the healing properties of more than three hundred herbs, many of which are still used in medicine today. Ayurveda, the Indian practice of preventing disease by balancing the various energies of the body, also started calling on herbs thousands of years ago. Around 800 BC, one of the first precursors to the modern hospital was founded in India, its shelves stocked with thousands of herbs, from the obscure (shatavari root, guduchi stem) to the familiar (licorice, ashwagandha).

The process of deciding what plant to use for which ailment was largely experimental, though an herb's outer form—its color, scent, or shape—often spoke to the cure it held within. Herbs used to treat jaundice, for instance, often had yellow flowers, mirroring the shade of a patient's skin when he or she was infected with the disease. Pansies, on the other hand, were used for heart troubles because of their heart-shaped petals. The ancient spice trade spread these powerful herbs across Asia and the Mediterranean, where they took on immense cultural value. Many now-common herbs were prized rarities back then, and legend has it that certain soldiers used to be paid in salt, which led to the word "salary" and the phrase "worth his salt."

Throughout the years, plants were used in times of war and peace: Surgeons traveling with an army used herbs to treat battle wounds, and their flowers were featured in celebrations of nature and togetherness.

Beyond their practical uses, herbs, plants, flowers, and natural relics gained occult appeal over the years too. Since plants come from the earth, mystics often incorporated their grounding energy into spells and rituals. When Joan of Arc was accused of witchcraft, people used the fact that she carried mandrake root around with her as proof.

Today, herbs still hold immense value, especially in spiritual circles. You can't walk into a magic shop without being engulfed by the herbal scents of sage or sweetgrass—aromas associated with cleansing and positive energy. There's even something vaguely spiritual about the simple act of drinking tea—the steady steeping of flowers and herbs into water, the slow sipping of the earth.

FINDING THE RIGHT HERBS FOR YOU

Herbs are one of the most varied and versatile tools out there, so it may take a while to find the right ones for your needs.

Biodiverse regions are hotspots of wild plant medicine, and places such as the jungles of Costa Rica hold thousands of species, each touting its own unique properties. Like crystals, herbs tell the story of the unique lands from which they came. The first step is finding one that speaks to you; then you can decide how to use it. Plants can be consumed as tinctures and teas or applied topically, transformed into essential oils and aerosols, or set on fire and harnessed for their smoke.

For the purposes of this book, we will be using dried herbs for space clearings and teas, as well as fresh herbs and flowers for bathing and cleansing. While you can find dried and fresh plants at any grocery store, farmers market, or herbal remedies shop, you'll want to make sure they're high in quality and low in environmental impact. Grow them yourself, or look for organically grown or wildcrafted where possible. The latter are foraged straight from their native environments, so they shouldn't contain any chemical fertilizers or pesticides. We will mostly be using herbs topically, but when you are consuming them, be sure to do your research and start small to see how your system reacts.

HOW TO USE HERBS AND PLANTS

* **BURN AN HERBAL BUNDLE:** The smoke of dried sage, sweetgrass, or lavender, tied together with string, is thought to cleanse a space and impart it with positive energy, and cultures worldwide have harnessed this knowledge for centuries. The smoke can also be used to "clean" some of the other mystical tools you'll be working with, such as crystals and tarot decks.

* **START A TEA RITUAL:** By drinking your tea around the same time every day, you're signaling to your brain that it's time to wake up, calm down, or stay focused. Tea can also be used to promote togetherness,

and tea ceremonies with friends are wonderful opportunities to gather and do something different.

* **MAKE A TINCTURE**: Made by preserving plant material in alcohol, herbal tinctures are popular in the holistic healing community. Though usually not the best tasting, a few dropperfuls a day can help soothe anything from a stomachache to allergies to brain fog, depending on the herbs used. You can also ditch the alcohol and use the mixture as a beauty water to spray on your face for a quick refresh.
* **TRY A FACIAL STEAM**: There's nothing more luxurious than immersing yourself in a bed of flowers. Combine flowers, herbs, and hot water in a bowl, drape your face a few inches above the water line, and breathe.

RAPID—FIRE RITUALS

Here are a few of our favorite herbal rituals that can be completed in five minutes or less. Give them a try so you can become comfortable with the tool before diving into more involved seasonal rituals.

A SMUDGING FOR A FRESH START

1. Light the herbal bundle of your choice over a large shell, such as an abalone. This pulls in a water element, to complement the fire, earth, and air energies already in the mix. If you don't have a shell, you can use a small plate or bowl.
2. Immediately blow out the flame and waft the smoke around as you walk through your environment, repeating either internally or aloud, "Here is where I start anew."
3. After a few moments, let the smoke burn out or smother it in the shell.

You can complete this ritual over your entire home or even over a new purchase that you want to infuse with positivity before you begin using it. We tend to do this over new clothes, especially thrift shop finds, since they've lived an entire life before finding us.

AN INCENSE RITUAL FOR DEEP WORK

1. Incense sticks are another incredible herbal tool that you can find in most natural grocers or spiritual shops. Find a scent you like, and light it right before you need to get some work done.
2. As you light and blow out the flame, letting the smoke escape, visualize yourself completing the task ahead.
3. Fueled by the aromatic smoke, work without break until the incense stick has burned to its end.

During the process of writing this book, the lighting of an incense stick became a signal for us that it was time to get to work. We've found that it's especially clarifying first thing in the morning or late at night.

ESSENTIAL OILS

Scent is a powerful messenger, able to transport us to an entirely different time and place. Our brain chemistry allows for this journey. When you take a whiff of something, it travels up through the nose into the olfactory nerve of the brain. Once your brain processes a scent, it sends a signal to the amygdala and hippocampus, the regions that store emotions and memories. Visual, auditory, and tactile experiences don't pass through these same brain areas. That's why smells can unlock moments we thought we had long forgotten. In fact, scent memories have been found to stretch further back in time than the memories evoked by any other sense.

Scent can also change the way we experience the present moment. Anyone who has spent time on a smelly, suffocating subway car knows the instant reprieve that comes with that first whiff of fresh air when you step off. It's no wonder that aromatherapy is now the most popular alternative treatment for stress and anxiety worldwide.

One of the most effective ways to self-soothe with scent is by using essential oils. These oils are made using the highly concentrated active principle found in flowers, grasses, leaves, roots, and trees. These compounds are antiseptic, meaning they reduce the spread of infection, and they are responsible for giving plants their smells.

Extracting them is no easy task. Sixty thousand rose blossoms are used to produce one ounce of rose oil, jasmine flowers need to be picked on the first day they blossom in order to retain their olfactory power, and a sandalwood tree needs to be at least thirty years old—and thirty feet tall—before it can be tapped for oil. But the result is well worth the trouble. Essential oils are potent plant medicines that can be ingested or applied topically, diffused or sniffed straight from the vial. They can wake us up and calm us down, sharpen our minds and ease our pain, turning us into powerful alchemists with each unscrewing of the cap.

THE STORY OF ESSENTIAL OILS

Hippocrates, the Greek physician who has been called the father of medicine, said it best in his musing, "The way to health is to have an aromatic bath and scented massage every day." The cultures we mentioned earlier that first harnessed herbs for medicinal purposes were also at the forefront of scent exploration. Essential oils were popular in Ayurvedic practices and Chinese medicine, and they were also mentioned in the Bible upward of two hundred times. Ancient Egyptians, though, were the ones who really honed this healing tool. The masterful scent weavers famously used frankincense, myrrh, and sandalwood to soothe all hosts of wounds and buried embalmed bodies with essential oils to forge a connection between the deceased and the divine. Hints of blue lily have been found on mummified bodies, centuries after their initial journeys underground. Some of these historic scents still feel welcoming to us today, evoking holiday and tradition in their spicy, floral richness.

Through time, certain smells have also adapted romantic and spiritual personas. Consider stories such as Cleopatra luring Marc Antony to her bed with rose, and European physicians burning frankincense on the streets to ward off illness and evil spirits during the bubonic plague.

These dynamic uses have been immortalized in huge essential oil textbooks, one of the oldest being *Complete Herbal*, published in 1653. Information on

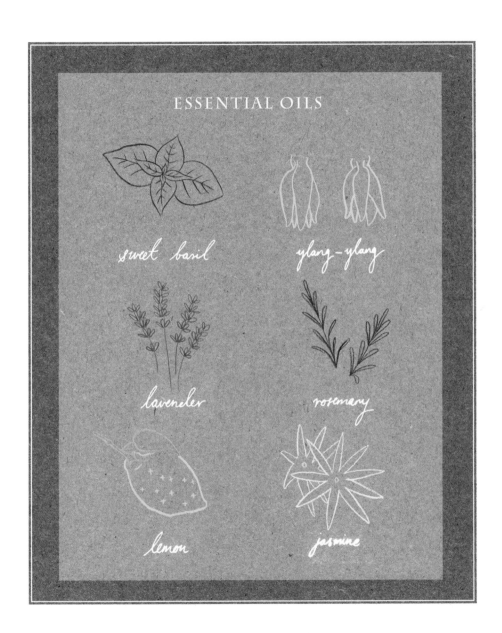

ESSENTIAL OILS

sweet basil

ylang-ylang

lavender

rosemary

lemon

jasmine

essential oils was far from new or novel even back then, though, which suggests that they are truly some of the oldest healers we have access to. When talking about the properties of the oils of chamomile flowers, author Nicholas Culpeper wrote, "It is so well known everywhere that it is but lost time and labor to describe it."

AN OIL FOR EVERY MOOD

Nowadays, there are upward of three hundred essential oils in circulation, all of which have their own unique properties. Here are a few notable ones for every mood:

If you need to calm a racing mind

Bergamot

Jasmine

Sandalwood

Ylang-ylang

If you need to focus

Pine

Peppermint

Rosemary

Cedarwood

If you need energy

Cajeput

Sweet basil

Citrus (grapefruit, lemon, lime, mandarin, etc.)

Spearmint and peppermint

If you need to sleep

Lavender

Vetiver

Roman chamomile

Frankincense

FINDING THE RIGHT ESSENTIAL OIL FOR YOU

This may seem obvious, but before you invest in an oil, you should make sure you actually enjoy its scent. Don't decide based on healing pedigree alone! Just like certain scents can transport us to joyful places right away, one sniff of others can instantly ruin our mood.

Another thing to keep in mind is that there's often a large price discrepancy between oils, since some are much more difficult to extract. A single ounce of rose otto retails for $400 or more, while scents such as lavender, tea tree, and citruses will set you back only a few bucks. If you're just getting started, it's probably a good idea to go with less expensive scents and work your way up to more luxurious ones.

No matter what type of oil you are in the market for, make sure it's high in quality. Some manufacturers dilute their oils or create them in a lab instead of extracting them from plants, and while these blends may smell just as good, they don't pack the same healing benefits. Sometimes the nose alone can't tell a real from a phony, so it's worth it to look into the manufacturer. If a label lists both an oil's common name and its Latin one, its country of origin, and a certified organic designation, it's a good sign. Ignore the "grade" of the oil, as this isn't regulated, and go for small-batch producers whenever possible.

Store your oils in a cool, dry place so they stay potent longer, and house them in glass containers, not plastic ones. Oils can actually draw out the chemicals in plastic, which makes them less fragrant and unsafe to use in some cases.

A NOTE ON SAFE APPLICATION

* When trying out a new scent, use your hand to waft a bit into your nose instead of inhaling straight from the bottle. Directly sniffing a fragrance you don't enjoy can be really unpleasant.

* Before applying oils to your skin, first make sure that they are safe for topical application. (Some aren't, and a quick Google search will tell you if that's the

case.) Then, combine them with a carrier oil such as jojoba, coconut, or grapeseed at a ratio of at least five drops of carrier oil to one drop of essential oil. While some oils can be applied neat (without a carrier), it's always better to err on the side of caution and patch test to see how your skin reacts.

* If you have extra-sensitive skin, apply oils to the soles of your feet first, as the skin there is stronger.
* If you want to remove an irritating oil from the skin, thoroughly scrub with a carrier oil and water until it washes off.
* Do not go out into direct sunlight after applying oils, especially citrus ones. It can cause temporary redness, irritation, or darkening of skin.

HOW TO USE ESSENTIAL OILS

* **CREATE YOUR OWN BLEND**: Grab a glass bottle, carrier oil, and a few pleasing fragrances and see what concoctions you can create. Mixing your own blend is a fun way to play around with scent, and the results can become go-to remedies when you're stuffed up, getting ready for sleep, or seeking focus.
* **DIFFUSE AN OIL**: Use essential oil diffusers to spread your favorite scent around a room. Diffuse for one to two hours at a time. Any longer and they tend to lose their potency.
* **WORK THEM INTO YOUR BEAUTY ROUTINE**: Oils come equipped with impressive cosmetic benefits—able to do everything from nourish dry skin to soothe bug bites—so you can DIY a cleanser or moisturizer that's tailored to your specific wants and needs.

RAPID—FIRE RITUALS

Here are a few of our favorite smell-good rituals that can be completed in five minutes or less. Give them a try so you can become comfortable with the tool before diving into more involved seasonal rituals.

AN AROMATHERAPY RITUAL FOR ENERGY

1. Combine a few energizing scents (we're partial to lemon and lime) into two glass carriers until you have blends that are pleasing to your nose.
2. Place one of your bottles at your desk or wherever you tend to work. Place the other in your bag or whatever you carry around throughout your day.
3. Every time you're lacking energy, inhale for a few seconds in each nostril, closing your eyes and picturing the scents invigorating both sides of the brain. This is also a great tool for travel.

Emma has taken on the reputation of a lemon oil pusher—she'll carry a vial to work and pass it on to anyone who seems stressed, exhausted, or in low spirits.

A BLENDED BALM RITUAL FOR GOOD HEALTH

1. Dilute a few drops of eucalyptus into a carrier oil and combine with beeswax over the stove on low heat until melted.
2. Pour into a glass container with a wide opening and allow to cool and harden.
3. Whenever you feel sniffly, headachy, or just generally sick before bed, massage the balm into your chest and forehead (testing in a small patch first). Take in deep breaths of the scent as you picture it extracting any pains from your body.

Ever the solution to stuffiness, we liken this to the holistic application of the Vicks rub our parents used to put on us as kids. In that way, it's comforting in its familiarity.

Astrology

One of humanity's earliest ways to classify the sky above, astrology feels more potent and pervasive today than ever before.

For some, it means horoscopes—daily, weekly, and monthly projections that promise predictability in an increasingly chaotic world. Listening to what the zodiac has to say about your sign's tendencies at once removes us from our lives and thrusts us into them—offering a concise explanation for things that are not easily put into words.

But if you're exploring astrology only to see what kind of week you're going to have or how compatible you are with your significant other, you're not using this tool to its full potential. Reading your natal chart, which illustrates the position of the planets in the moment of your first breath, is a much deeper, more nuanced dive into the cosmic forces at play in your life. The chart goes beyond your sun sign (the one that is used in traditional horoscopes) and uses the celestial snapshot to pull in dozens of other little insights into your character.

At its simplest, astrology is a tool that pushes you to think about yourself and your spirit. It forces you to consider things like how you process emotion, why you may unconsciously gravitate toward certain people, and what you need to feel fulfilled. Despite their importance, we often don't think about these traits in the go-go-go of our daily routines. When's the last time a doctor asked you to rate your emotional intelligence on a scale of 1 to 10 or a job application prompted you to describe your most recent intuitive hit?

From a pragmatic standpoint, approaching your life through the lens of astrology can yield insights into your personality you wouldn't have found otherwise. And from a more metaphysical perspective, reading your chart is a reminder that human experience is in part dictated by the galaxy. Plus, there's something comforting in the simplicity of it all—the idea that, through times of peace and war, chaos and calm, humanity can fall into twelve little boxes.

THE STORY OF ASTROLOGY

The foundations of astrology started in ancient Babylonia, where diviners would look to patterns in nature to explain what was going on around them, operating off the idea that the gods put clues about the future in places where they knew humans could find them. This philosophy inspired the Greeks to give name to the zodiac as we know it today with the term *zodiakos kyklos*, or animal circle. They then further developed the twelve signs by assigning them to animals and gods. Aries took on the mascot of a ram—a reference to the myth of a golden ram that saved two royal children from being sacrificed. Leo became a lion—an animal that Hercules once had to conquer to atone for his past mistakes.

Greek philosopher Pythagoras then helped shape the personal significance of astrology by theorizing that every human contained the universe and that our bodies were merely vessels through which the cosmos could shine. References to this idea dotted literature and art for centuries to follow. Dante's *The Divine Comedy*, a long-form poem from fourteenth-century Italy, traces the journey of the soul through different planets until it reaches Paradise.

The height of the astrological practice probably came in Renaissance Europe, when textbooks were dedicated to it, professors taught it in university, and King Henry VII kicked off the trend of royalty consulting with in-house astrologers to plan and plot. Especially through periods of conflict and war, diviners were sought after for their prophesies. Over time, though, the lack of support for astrology by some scientific and religious communities (if the future was dictated by the stars, where did God fit in?) caused it to fade in and out of public consciousness.

Astrology as we know it today emerged with a reporter named R. H. Naylor. In the 1930s, Naylor, a Brit, shadowed an old shaman and astrologer, known as Cheiro, who read the palms of celebrities (Mark Twain, Grover Cleveland, and Winston Churchill were all rumored to have been clients). Naylor translated the mystical knowledge he picked up along the way into the first real newspaper horoscope: a reading for the newest member of the

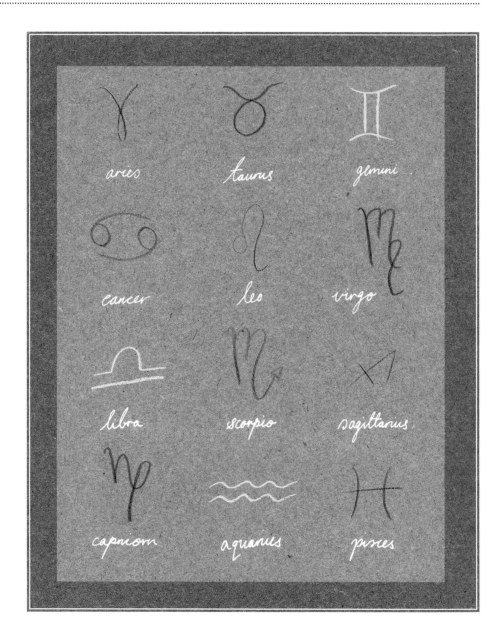

royal family, Princess Margaret, in *The Sunday Express*. Readers far and wide eagerly consumed her chart, which inspired Naylor to dedicate an entire column to astrology. Legend has it that he became a household name after one of his articles accurately predicted the crash of a British airplane. Soon enough, other publications sought to mimic his success with horoscopes of their own.

HOW TO DECODE YOUR ASTROLOGY

At first glance, your natal chart is a hodgepodge of shapes, symbols, and numbers. While you could easily fill a whole book with tips on how to decipher your chart (and many have), here is a quick primer on how to decode it.

1. **THE BIG THREE**: Three of the most important personality indicators are the zodiac signs that your sun, moon, and ascendant fall into. The sun sign, the one most prominent in Western astrology, represents your identity and external need for validation. Your moon sign, on the other hand, speaks to your subconscious, your true nature, which gives rise to deeply rooted needs and emotions. Its feminine energy balances your sun sign's masculine one, and it's the inner root of your outward persona. Your ascendant, rising sign—the constellation that was on the horizon when you were born—symbolizes how you come off to others and how you are ascending toward your life's mission.

2. **THE PLANETS**: The eight planets surrounding Earth (yes, Pluto still counts) fall into signs on your chart as well. Each one governs how you experience certain aspects of the world, such as how you communicate (Mercury), deal with power (Pluto), and fulfill your life's purpose (Saturn). Each zodiac sign corresponds to a particular planet. Your almighty "ruling planet" is the one associated with your rising sign. If you're a Virgo rising, your chart's ruling planet is Mercury, and you'll likely be more affected by Mercury's orbit and movements.

3. **NORTH AND SOUTH NODES**: The north and south nodes of the moon (the points where it enters an eclipse) lie directly across from each other on your chart. The north node speaks to your destiny, and the south node represents what you're working to shed over your lifetime—the not-so-positive patterns you're hoping to leave behind.

4. **THE HOUSES**: Your natal chart is divided into twelve houses. Think of each one as a piece of the astrological pie. The houses that your sun, moon, planets, and nodes were passing through when you were born dictate where their qualities are likely to manifest. There's a house for family, home, finances, etc. They build off one another until they converge in the twelfth house and break down once again. So if your Leo sun sign falls into the fifth house (which speaks to romance), you might show off your creative, curious nature most in your relationships. If your north node lies in the third house (communication), you may be destined to become a respected author.

Here's a breakdown of all the houses:

1st:	identity, self, well-being, and personality
2nd:	self-esteem, how you value yourself, earned income
3rd:	self-expression, communication, early childhood development
4th:	safety and security in the world, family
5th:	cocreation, romance, fun, creativity, children
6th:	health, stability, daily routines, day-to-day work
7th:	contractual relationships such as marriage, business relationships, and contracts
8th:	transformation, shared resources
9th:	religion, worldview, higher education, international travel
10th:	prestige, esteem, how you are seen and respected, career success
11th:	hopes and wishes, manifestation, groups and friends
12th:	disintegration for reinvention, spirituality, shedding of the unconscious

And then there are the qualities of every sign. For us, comparing the energy of a sign to that of a season in the northern hemisphere makes a lot of sense. Everyone knows about the feelings that the year's cycles conjure, and it's easy to believe the idea that you take on some of the traits of the particular season you were born into.

ARIES (MARCH 21–APRIL 19, FIRE): The first sign of the zodiac, Aries is a fearless leader. Aries season falls at the start of spring, when the world is first starting to regain some of the ram's signature fire. Like the first leaves to reappear on the trees, the sign is showy, colorful, and lush.

TAURUS (APRIL 20–MAY 20, EARTH): Taurus season is about appreciating the new bounties of spring. The earth sign is grounded and grateful for the finer things in life. Think picnics, long walks outdoors, and fresh flowers.

GEMINI (MAY 21–JUNE 20, AIR): Master communicators, Geminis are fueled by a curiosity about anything and everything. They'll travel near and far seeking out new stories and experiences, so it makes sense this sign falls during the kickoff of summer break.

CANCER (JUNE 21–JULY 22, WATER): Cancer comes at the start of summer, with an energy that is highly emotional, intuitive, and sentimental. The sign speaks to the longing for home that sets in during a vacation, the desire for familiarity that hits in a foreign place.

LEO (JULY 23–AUGUST 22, FIRE): As the height of summer hits, Leo emerges as the zodiac's showy creative. This expressive fire sign is a bold leader, fueled by the heat and energy of the season.

VIRGO (AUGUST 23–SEPTEMBER 22, EARTH): As summer crawls to an end and we all sober up from its riches, Virgo energy helps us get our lives back in order. The organized, detail-oriented sign of the zodiac, it signals a return to school and work.

LIBRA (SEPTEMBER 23–OCTOBER 22, AIR): Libra is represented by the scales, as the sign chases equity and fairness for everyone. As we move further into the fall season, themes of such balance emerge. We start to live our lives inside and outside and dip our toes into the introspection of winter while still holding on to some of summer's outward-facing energy.

SCORPIO (OCTOBER 23–NOVEMBER 21, WATER): Scorpio season signals the first plummet into colder weather and longer nights. The sign is the zodiac's ultimate mystery, and it isn't afraid to reckon with darker topics like death, loss, and power struggles.

SAGITTARIUS (NOVEMBER 22–DECEMBER 21, FIRE): Sagittarius is a sign of dreamers. Once we have embraced the darkness of fall, the sign beckons us to get out and explore it, so it's fitting that it falls during a time of social gatherings like Thanksgiving and holiday parties.

CAPRICORN (DECEMBER 22–JANUARY 19, EARTH): Capricorn is the wise, practical doer of the zodiac. Capricorn season falls around the calendar new year, helping us set and stick to our resolutions.

AQUARIUS (JANUARY 20–FEBRUARY 18, AIR): As we near the end of the zodiac, Aquarius emerges as the great uniter. It brings together all the signs that preceded it so that we can move onto something greater as a collective whole.

PISCES (FEBRUARY 19–MARCH 20, WATER): The final sign of the zodiac, Pisces brings about a reflective, esoteric energy. It signals the end but also the beginning—bringing us forward into a new season and new opportunity to cycle through the zodiac's expanses.

MAKING ASTROLOGY WORK FOR YOU

We see astrology as a means of exploring your inherent energy and inclinations. But we also know that free will is very real. While it's always fun to read about what could be "written in the stars" for you, at the end of the day, the trajectory of our lives is largely shaped by our environment and experience. Most astrologers will tell you the same thing. This explains why twins can have identical natal charts but distinct personalities and why those born during the same time of year can go on to have such wildly different life experiences.

We recommend using astrology as a lens through which to consider what makes you, you—the wants, needs, desires, quirks, and quips that stay constant when everything around you is changing.

HOW TO USE ASTROLOGY

* **HAVE A CHART READING.** You can access your natal chart online, as long as you know the time and place you were born. If you're new to astrology, having your chart read by an expert can open up a ton of new insights you might not have noticed on your own.
* **PRACTICE READING A FRIEND'S CHART.** When you start to get a handle on your own chart, you can use this newfound language to analyze the charts of friends and family, which is always a lot of fun.

RAPID-FIRE RITUALS

Here are a few of our favorite zodiac rituals that can be completed in five minutes or less. Give them a try so you can become comfortable with the tool before diving into more involved seasonal rituals.

AN ASTRO READING RITUAL FOR BALANCE

1. Look at the "big three" elements of your chart—your sun, moon, and rising signs—and see what element they're in.
2. Then, write down any elements your chart is lacking. Are your sun, moon, and rising signs mostly fire signs, with water to be found nowhere? Do you have a lot of earth but no air?
3. Moving forward, consider adding more activities that correspond with the element you're lacking and see if you can feel any gaps filling.
   a. Water: Watch a movie that makes you cry.
   b. Air: Write a letter to someone you love.
   c. Earth: Head out into nature barefoot.
   d. Fire: Try a new type of exercise.

EMMA IS A GEMINI SUN, an air sign; a Leo moon, a fire sign; and a Virgo rising, an earth sign. The lack of water in her chart means she could use some help sitting with and processing her emotions. She's working on it. Lindsay is a Leo sun sign but only by twenty-two minutes. She's right on the cusp of Cancer and Leo. With her moon in Cancer and Scorpio rising, her chart is full of fire and water signs, which are often at odds with each other. They allow her to have soft intensity at best, but it's easy to fall out of balance with one or the other. A regular yoga practice keeps her in check.

1. The night of a full moon, think about your moon sign's preferred mode of communication. Are you a chatty Gemini, a showy Leo?
2. Tailor your full moon ritual (more on those on page 34) to your astrology and see if it changes how you connect to the energy of the night.

TAROT

For those who haven't used them before, tarot cards may conjure images of a psychic reading—a dark, mysterious room aglow with candles, incense, and a crystal ball or two. In reality, tarot is much more than a fringe divination tool. The deck of seventy-eight cards prompts you to tap into your intuition and inner knowing. Think of it like a wise friend or loved one—a confidant who encourages you to trust yourself above all else.

THE STORY OF TAROT

Long ago, tarot cards were used purely for entertainment. The first iteration of tarot arrived in the fifteenth century by way of Italy, when artists created a new type of deck for card games. As time passed, the wealthy began commissioning special decks with more detailed, lifelike imagery set against regal gold backdrops. These tiny works of Renaissance art formed the basis of the deck we use today, with twenty-two Major Arcana cards, which represent larger-than-life spiritual moments with figures like the sun and the devil, and fifty-six Minor Arcana cards, which provide smaller snapshots into everyday life.

As their imagery and verbiage grew more sophisticated, the cards also picked up more spiritual meaning. The tarot reached a pivotal moment when Arthur Edward Waite, a British poet and scholarly mystic, asked artist Pamela Colman Smith to illustrate a deck to accompany his book *The Pictorial Key to the Tarot* in 1909. The result was the Rider-Waite deck—a collection of cards that is at once realistic and otherworldly, featuring royalty immersed in mystical landscapes. It was the first tarot deck to be mass-produced in English, and it became the inspiration for most cards you'll find on the market today.

FINDING THE RIGHT DECK FOR YOU

Traditionalists may be tempted to kick off their tarot journey with the classic Rider-Waite deck, but be warned that these cards can read a little dark. While there are no inherently "bad" cards in tarot, pulling a horned, fiery devil when you're just getting started can be disheartening, so we recommend starting with a deck that is a little softer—especially if you're prone to worry. Thankfully, there are tarot and oracle decks that appeal to every taste. Oracle decks are meant to be used in the same way as tarot, but they have different themes and may not have exactly seventy-eight cards. Some speak to the time they were created (the Morgan-Greer is a colorful depiction of the 1970s); others, to the people who may use them (the Dust II Onyx depicts women of color on every card); and others, to a certain aesthetic (the Minimalist Oracle is an interpretation of tarot's detailed scenes as colorful shapes).

There's an old superstition that instead of choosing your own deck, you need to wait until one finds you: Someone gifts it to you, you stumble across it by accident, or it falls into your life in some other way that's beyond your control. While there's certainly something to be said for treating your deck like a present from the universe, you'll still find plenty of people buying their own, so no shame in doing so when the time is right. When you're looking for a deck that resonates with you, let your intuition be your guide. What cards are you drawn to right away? Since your deck will become a very personal, sacred tool, it's best to go with one with imagery that really speaks to you, even if you can't reason exactly why.

When you get a new deck, you should use sage to cleanse its energy, as you did with your crystals. As you waft smoke around your cards, program them to speak to your life and experience. Take them in your hands and envision that your touch is further tailoring their messages to you. Then, shuffle the cards well, get used to the feeling of holding them, and prepare for your first pull.

Simply sit down and pick a card, any card. Place it facedown on a flat surface first; then turn it around. If you draw one you're not pleased with, don't just return it to the pile. Look in the guidebook that comes with your cards and read through what it has to say about your pull. The power then comes in placing each card within the context of your life, so think about what it could be trying to tell you in that moment. Trust your gut. Grab a pen and let the words flow onto a page if that's helpful. Don't dwell on any card for too long. Intuition only dulls with time, and your first thought is probably the most valuable, no matter how "out there" it may feel. In fact, the weirder, the better. People follow the same logical paths all the time, and they all usually end in the same place. It's the unpaved trails, the ones that seem foreign and mysterious and scary, that you're trying to find with this exercise. It's the card interpretations that come deep from the belly that are packed with spirit, not the ones that are mass-produced in the logical mind.

As for when to do a pull, that's entirely up to you. The rules of tarot are loose, and they basically just say to honor and trust the cards. You can pull one card every single morning or do a three-card spread once a month. You can journal about a pull for hours or forget about it in five minutes. We like to turn to the deck when we are stuck or unsure how to move forward with a problem, looking to it almost as we would a trusted friend who can lend advice we wouldn't have otherwise come across. Again, it's all about intuition here. If you have the distinct feeling that something—anything—is missing, like there is some sort of message that is waiting to shine through but hasn't quite peeked above the clouds, try tarot to get clear. If you are going through a transitional period and don't know what it will take to get through to the other side unscathed, grab a card and see what it offers up to you. Like astrology, we see tarot as a conduit for fresh, unique thoughts. But while astrology is more focused on your inner landscape, tarot is more outward facing and action oriented.

Once you get into a routine of using your deck consistently, something semi-magical will happen. The cards you pull will start to speak louder and louder, somehow becoming more resonant and applicable in that moment.

They will leave you at once smiling and nodding and shaking your head and knowing and trusting. This power is twofold: It's partially you becoming a more intuitive being, able to find and follow your inner voice, and maybe— just maybe—it's your cards getting to know you too.

HOW TO USE TAROT

* **PULL A SINGLE CARD.** Pull a card from your deck whenever you feel called, thinking first about a question you'd like answered.
* **DO A MULTI-CARD SPREAD.** You can also pull spreads that involve multiple cards. Powerful three-card pulls include a spread that speaks to past, present, and future and one for the energy of a problem, its cause, and its solution.

RAPID-FIRE RITUALS

Here are a few of our favorite tarot rituals that can be completed in five minutes or less. Give them a try so you can become comfortable with the tool before diving into more involved seasonal rituals.

A SINGLE-CARD PULL FOR SUPPORT

1. At the start of a new chapter in life, let your intuition lead you to one card. It can be a new job, a new city, or just a new moon.
2. Think about the message it could be sending you, then place it in your wallet or somewhere else you know you will see it every day.

When starting a new job, Emma pulled a card from an oracle deck that depicts a woman walking under the moon and reads, "I trust the mysteries of life." Every time she sees this in her wallet, she remembers to cut herself some slack and trust the universe to help her out.

A JOURNALING RITUAL FOR SELF-REFLECTION

1. First thing in the morning, pull a card that will speak to the day ahead.
2. Set a timer for three minutes and journal on what the card is saying to you, stream-of-consciousness style.
3. Look back on the writing later that night and see if it proved true.

We've always been inspired by those who are able to get into the habit of doing this every single morning to set the tone for the day.

BREATHWORK AND MEDITATION

Connecting with the breath is an accessible wellness tool anyone can use at any time. In yoga, we call breathwork *pranayama* (you might hear it called "pranayam" in yoga or meditation; that's a shorthand version). In the yogic lineages, *pranayama* is one of the eight limbs of Ashtanga yoga per the Yoga Sutras of Patanjali, the ancient text that's referenced time and again as the backbone of our modern yoga practice (verse 2:29). It's always been an integral part of yoga practice, but its therapeutic value is now being revealed to scientists and laypeople.

The breath is the only bodily function we can participate in—digestion, detoxification, and our heartbeat are all automatic. On principle, then, the breath is a space where our consciousness and subconsciousness meet.

Breathwork and meditation are not the same, but they work hand in hand. Breathwork can be construed as its own type of meditation. To be sure, manipulating the breath through measured exercises and patterns is a shortcut to a meditative state. A regular breathwork or *pranayama* practice can shift our state of being, and often that's the goal of both.

Meditation, on the other hand, has come to mean many different things to many different people. A mind-clearing activity such as running, painting, or even something as mundane as gift wrapping can be meditative—and for some that's enough. For others who crave more structure and a deeper self-study, there are several developed meditation techniques, with mindfulness meditation as the most prevalent today. Mindfulness meditation simply means sitting quietly, noticing your thoughts, and using your sense organs to become aware of what is happening in the present moment.

In the past half decade, we've enjoyed a surge of interest in Kundalini yoga, which uses breathwork and meditation as integral parts of the practice, but you can incorporate breathwork into any yoga practice. In fact, Lindsay enjoys a *pranayama* practice to open her daily morning meditation. As someone who suffers from asthma, she enjoys the feeling of pumping air through her lungs and benefits from the mind-clearing effects increased airflow begets.

Whether you're seeking support through a transition or a new practice to help complement meditation, yoga, journaling, or other self-care, the breath is a crucial ally.

THE SCIENCE OF BREATH

With modern technology, scientists have been able to unveil why people continue to come back to these practices again and again. For example, when regimented breathwork is paired with abdominal strength exercises, it's been shown to help people get unstuck—literally. A small-scale study examined the effectiveness of laxatives and a combination therapy of breathwork, ab exercises, and laxatives on a group of chronically constipated people and found that the ones who did diaphragmatic breathing moved things along more frequently than those who only took laxatives.

Another study done in the nineties shows how breathwork can be a therapeutic treatment for people with balance disorders, bringing a sense of equilibrium. Three groups of people were asked to move their bodies along with a changing graphic that was projected on a screen. People with experience in breathwork, both beginners and advanced practitioners, outperformed those without it.

A comprehensive, large-scale academic review of a specific system of breathwork (Sudarshan Kriya yoga) shows that it's a "low-risk, low-cost adjunct to the treatment of stress, anxiety, post-traumatic stress disorder, depression, stress-related medical illnesses, substance abuse, and rehabilitation of criminal offenders."

Holotropic breathwork, a specific system founded by Dr. Stan Grof that engages the diaphragm for full, quick breaths to flood the system with oxygen, has been shown to help mental health patients with particularly difficult issues when psychotherapy is failing. Other research links a regular breathwork practice with increased positive character traits, decreased negative ones, and an overall boost in self-awareness. Breathwork of all kinds is also used in addiction recovery programs across the world.

HOW TO USE BREATHWORK AND MEDITATION

* **A PRIMER FOR MEDITATION.** Use a breathwork technique to bring yourself out of your thinking mind and into present-moment awareness. Sit down and bring your attention to your breath. Without judgment, observe the feeling of your inhales and exhales as they move through you. This will quiet and focus your mind for meditation.
* **MOVE STAGNANT ENERGY.** Change your baseline state by revving yourself up with a fast, demanding breath exercise (e.g., *kapalabhati*) or slow it down with a cooling one (*sitali* or equal parts breath). Both of these techniques are described in the next section.

RAPID—FIRE RITUALS

Here are a couple of breathwork rituals you can do anytime, anywhere. You'll find more peppered throughout these pages.

SITALI: A COOLING BREATH

Sitali is a calming, cooling technique to use when it's hot, when you're feeling anxious, or when your emotional state is heated. This takes two to three minutes total.

1. Find a comfortable seat, breathing normally as you get centered. Then, curl your tongue and stick it out with your lips wrapped around it.
2. Breathe through your tongue only, feeling how the passage of air over your tongue causes evaporation and, subsequently, a cooling feeling. Continue like this on a three-count inhale and exhale.
3. Return to normal breathing.

BHASTRIKA (OR BELLOWS) BREATH: A HEATING BREATH

Bhastrika breath or bellows breath will build some heat in the body. If you need a reset, some warmth in the cold winter months, or mental clarity, try bellows.

1. Find a comfortable seat, breathing normally as you get centered. Begin breathing through your diaphragm by expanding your belly on the inhale and bringing your navel to your spine on the exhale.
2. Breathing only through your nose, make your inhales and exhales more forceful and of equal length. Do this for ten counts.
3. Breathe normally, and do one more round, increasing your count if you are experienced and it's desired.

Meditation and breathwork are both cumulative practices. It's always better to opt for a short practice than to skip it all together. With consistency and discipline, the combination is—dare we say—life-changing.

THE MOON AND THE SUN

Emma remembers the first time she realized we were all living under the same sky. When she was young, she thought that the sun, moon, stars, and planets followed her and her alone—staples in her backyard, passengers on her long family car trips, something that she could always find, just as they always found her. Then, she was told that her sky was shared and not hers alone, that someone thousands of miles away could be looking up at the same sun and moon. This realization that her steady companions were visiting everyone else too came as a surprise to her. She hopes that after the initial shock of it all, she was happy to learn this. And if not happy, at least a little amazed.

How stunning is it that the moon is constantly disappearing in the sky, just to rebuild itself later; that the sun rises every morning, engulfing the earth in light and coloring in everything after a night of black and white? Even if in those moments it feels as though the world as we know it has ended, the sun somehow comes up once again the next morning, and with it the reminder that dawn does always find us—that time is constant and cyclical. The moon and sun are forces of magic and spirit and energy that we all get to see every single day—and yet we've become complacent to their grandeur.

It takes only a moment to notice—really notice—the sun and moon, to celebrate their presence like a child might. But in doing so, we can step outside of ourselves and marvel in the world that surrounds us.

THE STORY OF THE SKY

Tracing the moon and sun back to their origins takes a while. Scientists now estimate that the sun formed around 4.6 billion years ago, when a rotating cloud of gas and dust collapsed and condensed into an object of unparalleled energy and force. Its sheer size could fit a million Earths; its surface is about 10,000 degrees Fahrenheit; and it would take one hundred billion tons of dynamite every second to match its energy. Though it feels like a source of infinite light, the sun as we know it will last another five billion years or so, until it sheds its outer layers and its core cools and collapses into a black dwarf—an invisible area defined by its emptiness.

After the sun came the moon. New theories for its formation emerge every few years, but the most popular remains that Earth collided with another planet and the debris from the crash formed the moon. This could explain why the moon and Earth are similar but not identical in composition.

The moon appears to change shape in the night sky due to the way the sun's light hits it. On a full moon, the entire moon is illuminated, while on a new moon Earth sits between the moon and the sun, our planet's shadow making the moon almost disappear. In between, the moon moves around Earth and takes on different shapes due to this shadow in a cycle of waxing and waning. Since the moon's gravitational field always moves in a dance with Earth's, it pushes and pulls water, creating our tides.

Through the ebbs and flows of history, the sky's constant, reliable schedule has informed our own calendars. The moon completes its orbit every twenty-nine and a half days, and this was the original inspiration for the length of our months. (The words "moon" and "month" actually have similar roots.) The sun and moon were our timekeepers before watches, the forces our ancestors followed for growing and reaping and hunting—for survival.

Through time, some also believed that the full moon sends foreboding messages. The myth that the full moon could send us into a frenzy has been around since the Roman goddess of the moon, Luna, whose name inspired the words "lunacy" and "lunatic." The early medical community largely accepted the idea that the light of a full moon drove odd behavior. In some hospitals, psychiatric patients were shackled during those bright full-moon nights, and crimes committed during them were more likely to be forgiven. Aristotle proposed that this lunacy was due to the fact that the human body is mostly made of water, so like the tides, it is susceptible to stirring with the moon's energy. Another, more medically sound explanation is that the bright light of the full moon might have caused sleep disturbances and the ensuing erratic behavior. While not quite as pervasive today, moon mania is still feared by the superstitious. In fact, as recently as 2007, police departments in the UK sent out more officers on full-moon nights to deal with expected increases in crime.

Still today, many of us look upward for guidance on how to live down here on Earth. Biodynamic farmers (ones who work to honor the rhythms of nature) will often harvest aboveground plants on the full moon and belowground roots on the new moon, when the earth's subtle pull is greater than the sky's.

MAKING THE SKY WORK FOR YOU

Aside from its occasional frenzy, our sky is largely a force of awe—one that sets a beautiful backdrop for ritual work.

The sun, with its heat and friction and brilliance, begs us to move around and explore, while the moon politely invites us to get quiet and look within. Its dramatic phases lend cadence to busy lives. Full moons and new moons always come every two weeks, so we can use their arrival as reminders to check in with ourselves.

The new moon represents a blank slate, the start of a new cycle in the sky

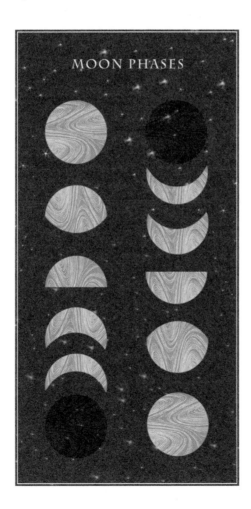

and here on Earth. It is therefore a time to set goals for the period ahead. New-moon nights are often defined by their low energy, and they may cause you to feel a bit sluggish. This is the moon's way of reminding you to slow down in body and mind, so you can get honest with yourself. The new moon is a time to manifest. It's a moment to commit to resolutions and continued growth. Decide what you want to call in, and then visualize that you already have it comfortably in your possession.

Two weeks later, the full moon represents the crest of a cycle. It's a period of intensity and power and commotion, when all things rise to the surface— whether we want them to or not. But when everything comes to light, it's easier to decide what is serving us and what isn't. Full-moon rituals, then, are a time to check in with your new-moon goals and release any negativity that may be keeping you from them, so you can finish out the lunar cycle strong.

By working in tandem with the sky, you can add consistency and regularity to your goal setting, which can only help.

SPECIAL LUNAR HOLIDAYS

Like the new moon and the full moon, special solar and lunar occasions are thought to emit their own power. Here are a few notable ones and how to welcome them.

Supermoon: A supermoon occurs when the moon sits closer to Earth on a new moon or full moon, thus appearing larger. It happens only a handful of times a year and amplifies the energy of new- and full-moon manifestations and releases.

Eclipse: Solar eclipses occur during new moons, when the moon sits between the sun and Earth and can block some light from the sun. Total solar eclipses, though rare, cause the sun to completely disappear from the sky for a moment in time, plunging the daytime into darkness. Considering the symbolism of the moon covering the sun, eclipses are a time to take some of the energy you would otherwise bring into the world and use it for inner work.

Equinox and solstice: A solar equinox occurs when the sun crosses the equator and the days and nights are equal in length. A solstice happens when the sun reaches its highest northern and southern points, making for the longest period of daylight and the longest night respectively in the northern hemisphere. Both signal a time to reflect on the season that has passed and plan for the new one ahead.

These days, who doesn't want to trust that the universe has their back in some big, intangible way? Just by existing, the moon is this huge force of magic, so the idea that it can send some of that energy down with its rays isn't so hard to believe after all.

HOW TO USE THE MOON AND THE SUN

* **USE THE FULL MOON TO FORGIVE**. Every full moon is a chance to metaphorically and physically drop anything that no longer serves you. You can write a letter saying good-bye to an old habit, rip up a piece of paper with negative self-talk written on it, etc.
* **HOST A MOON CIRCLE**. On a new moon or a full moon, invite some friends over to conduct a manifestation or release together. Holding space for one another to be raw and vulnerable can bring you together in a really powerful way and amplify the ritual's power.
* **TAILOR YOUR JOURNALING FOR THE NEW MOON**. Each moon phase corresponds with a zodiac sign, as the moon moves through that sign's energy. We can use the themes of each to help refine our visualizations and call in something new. Here are some questions to journal on for each one.
  * ARIES NEW MOON: What lights a fire under me and gets me excited? How can I do that more often?
  * TAURUS NEW MOON: What do I need to feel financially secure? How can I reframe my relationship with money for the better?

- GEMINI NEW MOON: When do I feel most authentically myself? What people can I surround myself with to feel like this more often?
- CANCER NEW MOON: How can I express my emotions in an authentic way?
- LEO NEW MOON: When do I feel most confident and self-assured? How can I get there more often?
- VIRGO NEW MOON: Is there anything in my life that feels chaotic? How can I get a better handle on it?
- LIBRA NEW MOON: When do I feel out of balance, emotionally or physically?
- SCORPIO NEW MOON: What is one friendship that I'd like to work on strengthening?
- SAGITTARIUS NEW MOON: How can I get out and experience something new this moon cycle?
- CAPRICORN NEW MOON: How can I shift my routine to feel more successful and fulfilled in my career?
- AQUARIUS NEW MOON: What's one time I helped enact positive change in my community? How can I get there again?
- PISCES NEW MOON: When do I feel most creative?

RAPID—FIRE RITUALS

Here are a few of our favorite lunar rituals that can be completed in five minutes or less. Give them a try so you can become comfortable working with the sky before diving into more involved seasonal rituals.

A FIRE RITUAL FOR RELEASE

1. On a full moon, think back on any negative energy or limiting beliefs keeping you from reaching a certain goal.
2. Write them down on small pieces of paper. Burn these little notes in a small fire, repeating the phrase "Thank you, but I no longer need you" with each one.

Since our New York City apartments don't have outdoor space, we've found that ripping up each piece of paper works well too—and doesn't set off any alarms.

A VISUALIZATION EXERCISE FOR CLARITY

1. Close your eyes and connect with your breath.
2. Once you settle in, begin to imagine yourself opening the door to your own personal paradise. What does this look like? What are you doing? Where are you? Who is around you? Don't judge anything you see—just observe.
3. Think about how this visualization can inspire your new-moon manifestations.

We've both conducted many visualizations like these and found that we never really know what paradise is going to look like on any given day. By setting the intention not to judge what comes up, you'll open yourself up to downloads that wouldn't have otherwise surfaced.

CRAFTING AN ALTAR TO STORE YOUR TOOLKIT

There's something to be said about setting aside space: space to grow, space to explore, space to discover. Altars provide that room to play, especially when used in tandem with ritual work.

The word "altar" is derived from a Latin word meaning "a high place," and altars were traditionally elevated on platforms. This etymology also speaks to the fact that altars can transcend all that is happening on Earth. In religion, altars have always offered a closer communion with the divine. They are mentioned dozens of times in the New Testament and continue to play a central role in sacred ceremonies and holidays around the world.

Regardless of your belief system, you can craft an altar that feels com-

fortable and inspiring. At their core, altars are spaces to slow down and get contemplative and quiet. Your altar doesn't need to be shiny or stately; it doesn't need to take up a whole room or even a whole shelf; and it doesn't need to be dressed up with crystals or constantly smell of sage. It can be as tiny as a corner of your closet and as unassuming as a stack of photos. The real beauty of an altar lies in your relationship to it; it's one place you can be unquestionably yourself.

Creating your altar should feel good, plain and simple. Think of it like an extension of those clusters of photos on your wall or collection of trinkets on your nightstand. It's a stage for you to tell a story.

Your altar can speak to a specific purpose or be a more general space where your spirit can come through. It can freeze the past by eternalizing someone who has passed away or celebrating an important moment like a wedding or birth, or it can speak to the future by depicting the sort of abundance you'd like to manifest in your life. It can be whatever you need it to be.

The first step in creating your display is deciding where to put it. It can take up a small area of the home if you're pressed for space or want to keep it discreet, but it should be somewhere that you pass every day. Maybe it's your bedroom, living room, or even backyard. You can place a cloth or trivet down to further spotlight the space and differentiate it from its surroundings.

From there, gradually add items that inspire you to slow down and start a dialogue with yourself. Maybe they drum up feel-good memories that put you in the mood to reflect or that remind you to devote a few moments to your breath.

⚜

ALTARS AROUND THE WORLD

The following are some ideas from a few of our favorite altars to get your wheels turning.

* Flowers, shells, or other elements representing nature (We love the idea of crafting an altar that is informed by the outdoors and changes with the season.)
* Photos of loved ones or of occasions you look back on fondly
* A trinket of your spirit animal (This can be an animal that you've always felt a special connection to, or one that seems to pop up in your life repeatedly.)
* A book you could read again and again
* A journal and a pen to record any thoughts that come to you as you're conducting your rituals

* A quote or a positive affirmation that fuels you
* A collection of tea lights or taper candles of different colors
* Meaningful jewelry, charms, or talismans
* A handwritten letter that you cherish
* Dried or fresh fruit to symbolize harvest and abundance
* A print from an artist you love or a sketch of your own creation

Remember that nothing on your altar needs to stay there forever. It's an evolution like anything else, so continue to check in from time to time to see if it still vibes with you. Likewise, feel free to add objects as you feel called.

HOW TO USE AN ALTAR

* **LET IT FUEL NEW HABITS**: Hoping to start a meditation practice? Set a cushion next to your altar and make it a space to sit and breathe every day. Want to start journaling? Place a notebook at your altar and write at least one word in it each morning, flipping over to a blank page afterward to remind yourself to do the same thing when you walk by the next day.
* **GATHER AROUND IT WITH FRIENDS**: Let your altar become a meeting place for any spiritual gatherings you hold with friends. You can encourage other people to bring something personal of their own to add, making the space feel communal.
* **CREATE A PORTABLE VERSION**: If you travel often, reserve a small box to house some of the trinkets on your altar when you're on the road.

Last but not least, we recommend making your altar the backdrop for most of the rituals outlined in this book. It's a great place to store your toolkit items: a tarot deck, your essential oil of choice, some sage for cleansing, etc. Using your altar as a space for ritual will imbue it with more meaning and memory, and you'll begin to associate it with some of the insights you glean over the coming pages.

Our hope for you is that through trying times, your altar can become enchantment embodied—a magical space among the mundane. May it serve as a source of inspiration to go out and conquer the world, as well as a quiet place to hide from it every once in a while.

And with that, it's time to start living with a little more spirit.

INTER

As above, so below; as within, so without;

as the universe, so the soul.

—HERMES TRISMEGISTUS

WINTER OFTEN GETS A BAD RAP. A season defined by darkness, its arrival beckons heavier coats, warmer fires, and longer sips of coffee. It replaces the vibrant hues of fall with a sharp, dreary landscape. The tips of branches newly bare whistle overhead, cold winds prickle the skin, and gray clouds mimic a collective energy that, from the outside, is drained of color. Yet underneath this veil of monotony, new life is building the strength to surface. Nature is having a little party underground—one that will become visible to us only with the passing of time. It's with the sudden flourish of spring's blossoms that we are reminded of the true theme of winter: hidden growth.

WINTER: A HISTORY

The winter solstice marks the astrological kickoff of the season, when the sun hangs its lowest in the sky and daylight is at its shortest.

Historically, the start of winter has brought with it a foreboding wave of challenges. A period of desolate farming and hunting conditions, winter's coming used to signal days spent rationing food supplies and fighting off the spread of disease for many. At the same time, the occasion also symbolized brighter moments to come. After all, once the sun reaches its lowest point, there's nowhere to go but up.

Cultures worldwide have joyfully acknowledged its arrival with celebration for centuries.

The Dongzhi festival in China marks the end of harvest, when families gather to consume warming, rich foods meant to raise their spirits for springtime. In Scandinavia, a multi-day feast marked the return of the sun god, and a massive bonfire welcomed her back in a flood of light. The solstice falls on the sun god's birthday in Persian tradition and is celebrated as the triumph of light over darkness. Families stay up for the longest night of the year in a ceremony known as Yalda, meaning "birth," retiring only when the sun has once again emerged victorious the next morning.

Reminders of the roots of these celebrations still lie in the earth's ruins. Ancient Egyptian temples face the solstice sunrise—the farthest south the sun ever rises—while BC-era geoglyphs (etchings of rocks and gravel) in Peruvian deserts align with this event. These landmarks transfer the purity, growth, and prosperity that are thought to be encapsulated in the winter sun's rays downward for us to harness.

THE SEASON'S SIGNIFICANCE

Under the Chinese five-element system, each element corresponds to a season (with early and late summer being split into two), so seasonal changes such as the solstice have far-reaching, profound effects. Winter is water—in all its engulfing, mysterious glory. It's a time to embrace stillness, celebrate sensitivities, let the tears flow, and address the senses that lie beneath the surface. It's a moment to look within, conserve energy, and take on the liquid's ability to mold to any vessel.

Energetically, winter is yin (feminine and fluid) as opposed to yang (masculine and domineering). It is a slow time to conserve your strength. According to Chinese medicine, water corresponds to the kidneys and bladder, which are linked to the systems that cleanse and moderate what we discard from the body. Metaphorically, this is our cue to gain clarity and get rid of anything that's not serving us.

It's also a time of profound planning. Similar to the new-moon phase, it is a blank canvas on which to manifest your intentions, get clear on what you want, and prepare to bring your dreams to life.

MODERN WINTER RITUAL

Today, holidays such as Christmas, Hanukkah, Chinese New Year, and Kwanzaa are celebrated in winter as occasions of togetherness and gratitude. Perhaps it's no coincidence that these gatherings come to us in this season, when we could all use a bit of social release with that inner work.

Modern New Year celebrations, on the other hand, have become largely ego-driven. While we're all for embarking on a journey to be your best self, listening to the season is paramount. Modern resolutions are too often imposed by commercial interests and out of touch with winter's ancient offering of going inward. We're doing ourselves a disservice if we're not reflecting, incubating, planning, and inquiring during the silence of winter.

It's a time to be inspired. In the most literal sense, the sharp chill in the air is invigorating and clarifies the mind. Being cold physically teaches us to sit with discomfort, to find calm, and to warm ourselves from the inside out. Even traditional winter sports like ice-skating and skiing are singular in nature, like a moving meditation asking us to find an inner rhythm.

WINTER IS A TIME TO . . .

* Slow down, reflect, and start this year from the inside out.
* Acknowledge where the past year has led you.
* Ask yourself what you really want to call into your life.
* Get in touch with your emotions by listening to music that makes you cry.
* Drink hot tea in bed.
* Make your home into a sweet spiritual sanctuary.
* Keep your inner world bright, no matter how harsh your outer one gets.
* Eat warming foods.
* Light candles—lots and lots of candles.

In many parts of the world, winter's short, frigid days and long, even colder nights can be quiet and lonely. They call on us to radiate our own warmth and sunshine, which requires some pretty intense self-reflection. So while winter may be a season to stand a bit more still, it's not an excuse to stop working. Instead, let's take its coming as a cue to gather our thoughts about the calendar year that's drawing to a close and plan how we'll navigate this next one.

A SAD SEASON?

The winter blues have taken on a more serious name in modern medicine: seasonal affective disorder (SAD). First identified by psychologist Norman Rosenthal in 1984, SAD is a cyclical depression that coincides with the seasons, usually peaking in the dead of winter. A combination of hormonal and circadian imbalances, it afflicts women four times more than men, and the farther north you live, the more susceptible you are. In America, 1 percent of Florida's population experiences SAD, compared to 9 percent of Alaska's.

Studies also show that SAD is a dance of environmental, biological, and psychological factors and that negative associations with the season can also spur symptoms. So what's the holistic equivalent to sunshine? Dr. Eva Selhub, a mind-body medicine expert and professor at Harvard Medical School, says it's a balanced, protein-heavy diet low in refined sugar and carbohydrates, plenty of exercise, and a daily vitamin D supplement. Getting enough sleep is important too, so she recommends going to sleep at the same time every night and leaving electronics out of the bedroom.

These winter rituals are all about inner rumination and quiet progress. They'll remind you that change takes time and nothing happens overnight, while also challenging you to discover and get to know a new part of you. Even more important, they'll teach you to be kinder to yourself, physically and emotionally, so you have the strength to wipe your slate clean and prepare for next year's work of art, knowing full well that it's going to be even more stunning than the last.

THE WINTER SOLSTICE

PLANT POWER

While the exact moment humans started domesticating plants is still debated, some scholars think that it all began in the hanging gardens of Babylon around 600 BC. Constructed by the Babylonian king Nebuchadnezzar II to appease his florally fixated queen, Amytis, the gardens brought bursts of greenery to an otherwise arid region. Believed to be a trove of terraces, columns, and palaces covered in cascading plants, it was one of the original seven wonders of the ancient world.

In Victorian-era England, plants reached another milestone. Spurred by an architectural shift toward stately bay windows and sun porches, homeowners began showcasing their plants indoors as status symbols. Botanical bounties abounded as scents of jasmine and citrus filled the air.

In the 1980s, NASA found that plants are more than just pleasing to the eye. They actually benefit our health by filtering out toxins like benzene, trichloroethylene, and formaldehyde in their quiet quest to create oxygen. If you look at photos of international space stations, you'll see that many of them actually have plants inside!

Once this research entered public consciousness in the eighties, indoor plants experienced another resurgence. Their popularity lulled in the nineties and has blossomed again only in the past ten years or so. Fast-forward to today and you can't go on social media without being greeted by a lush, looming fiddle-leaf fig, and windowsills without a succulent or two just seem dreary.

A PLANTING RITUAL FOR FAITH

Deep down into the burrows of winter we go with today's solstice. The new season brings with it an opportunity to slow down, check in, and set goals for the upcoming year.

This ritual asks you to call upon some potent plant power to clear the air in more ways than one. Tending to plants means finding faith in what lies beneath the surface—and eliminating some physical and metaphorical toxins from your life while you're at it.

WHAT YOU'LL NEED FROM THE OUTSIDE

* A pre-potted plant—or one from seed, if you're feeling ambitious
* A small crystal

WHAT YOU'LL NEED FROM WITHIN

* An intention for the rest of the season
* The willingness to get your hands a little dirty

INSTRUCTIONS

1. Take a trip to your local florist and choose an indoor plant you love—making sure, of course, that it has a chance to thrive in your space. Great starter plants include pothos, snake, and ZZ plants for low light, and succulents, spider plants, and monstera (our personal favorite) for bright light.
2. Spend a few minutes thinking up a one- or two-word intention for the season that lies ahead. If nothing comes to mind right away, first write out a few of your goals for the season and ruminate on the themes that surface. Then, write out your wintertime word or words on a piece of paper.

3. Wrap the paper around a small crystal. Aventurine and turquoise are our top picks, with their earthy-green and ocean-blue hues, but choose any that resonate with you, referring to page 1. Hold your crystal bundle in your hands, and repeat your intention. Speak quietly at first and slowly grow louder with every encore. Visualize yourself living out your intention, picturing exactly what that would look like in different, real-life scenarios.

4. Bury the crystal bundle, along with the energy of this visualization, in the dirt. Place your plant on or near your altar.

5. Mindfully tend to your new plant baby every day, making a small ritual of opening your blinds to give it light each morning and closing them at the day's end to signal rest. With each watering and fiddling of the shades, picture that your intention is also being tended to. Like a flower in spring, believe that it will eventually blossom with your love and care.

Tending to plants means trusting in what lies beneath the surface and having faith that it will blossom at just the right time. Though your plant, and your intention, may be slow to sprout, it's this gradual pace that makes its eventual growth that much more exciting. After all, nothing worthwhile has ever bloomed overnight.

HOW TO KEEP IT GOING

Christopher Satch is a plant scientist at New York City's wildly popular plant shop the Sill. He's also the one who mans their help desk, fielding dozens of emails a day from confused customers wondering why their houseplants are dying. Here are the top mistakes he sees new plant parents make. Keep them in mind as you tend to your new plant pal through this season and those to come.

1. **A PLANT IS CHOSEN BASED OFF LOOKS, NOT PRACTICALITY.** Think about what works for your lifestyle and space. Yes, fiddle-leaf figs may

be beautiful, but do you really have time to commit to their laundry list of care instructions? A cactus will never thrive in a dark corner, no matter how cute it looks there at first!

2. **PLANTS AREN'T GIVEN ENOUGH LIGHT.** Plants actually feed off light, not food. If your plant is a fast grower, that means that it's a fast eater and requires plenty of sun. On the other hand, if it's slow to grow, it can probably thrive in lower lighting.

3. **PLANTS ARE OVER— OR UNDERWATERED.** Give your plant water only when the top few inches of soil feel dry to the touch.

4. **THEIR OWNERS FREAK OUT ABOUT EVERY IMPERFECTION.** Some people will assume that their plant died at the first sighting of a brown spot on a leaf. Don't fret; that's totally normal!

THE FIRST NEW MOON OF WINTER

STAR LIGHT, STAR BRIGHT

If you're lucky enough to be outside on a clear winter's night when the moon is at its dimmest, a blanket of stars will likely greet you. Therein lies the great irony of winter: The coldest season hosts the most show-stopping sky. We can thank the dry air, the long nights, and Earth's positioning in the galaxy, away from the bright Milky Way, for this cold-weather light show.

Through the ages, people have viewed stars as windows to a higher realm and used their otherworldly wisdom to guide decisions here on Earth. Native American tribes saw the Milky Way as the road dead souls pass through to heaven, the brightest stars being the campfires they lit along the way. Siberian tribes saw the stars as the barrier between our world and the heavens, little windows that could open to allow in a peek into the bright lights of beyond. In eighth century Britain, they were also imbued with magic and superstition. A falling star to someone's left meant misfortune, while one on the right was a sign of good things to come.

Ancient folklore warned that trying to count the eons of stars in the night sky led to years of bad luck, while wishing on a shooting star was one way to ensure that the gods were listening to your every desire. Alchemists of the eighteenth century took on a more metaphysical view of them, believing that our souls dwelled in the bright twinkly lights. This last one is extra poetic in our eyes, especially when you remember that a star's light is visible only in the darkness. It makes sense, then, that the long, full nights of winter are the perfect time for our souls, our innermost selves, to shine together in a chorus of light.

Whatever your associations with the stars may be, you can probably find something magical about the night sky. It's a playground for our fantasies that, like all enticing things in life, is shrouded in a veil of mystery.

A STARGAZING RITUAL FOR RADIANCE

The new moon is a blank slate, an opportunity to set fresh intentions. Tonight, let's call on the stars to shed some light on how to move forward into the winter season. With this simple ritual, you can explore the sky on your own terms, allowing the cosmos to illuminate next steps.

WHAT YOU'LL NEED FROM THE OUTSIDE

* A blanket or dry surface to lie on
* A flashlight
* Warm clothes if you live in a colder region

WHAT YOU'LL NEED FROM WITHIN

* A commitment to braving the outdoors if you live in a cold area (We promise, it'll be worth it.)

INSTRUCTIONS

1. Find an isolated place to lie down, preferably on a hill or elevated surface so buildings and lights don't spoil your view.
2. Look up into the night sky, allowing your mind to wander wherever it wants. As you gaze at the stars and take in all the energy of our universe, feel the ground supporting you. Picture it infusing you with all the strength and power of history. Remind yourself of those who have walked it before you and those who will do so after you.
3. Shut your eyes. Close the curtain on the bright sky above and see what stars linger under your eyelids. Resist the urge to label or assign names to the constellations you see. Simply use them as reminders of the vast world out there and the physical space you hold within it. Acknowledge your inner universe behind the darkness of your eyelids, as expansive and awesome as the outer one you've just experienced.

4. Take out your flashlight and place it next to you, facing up toward the sky. Let it be a reminder that you are a source of your own light, a meaningful player in this cosmic dance of life.

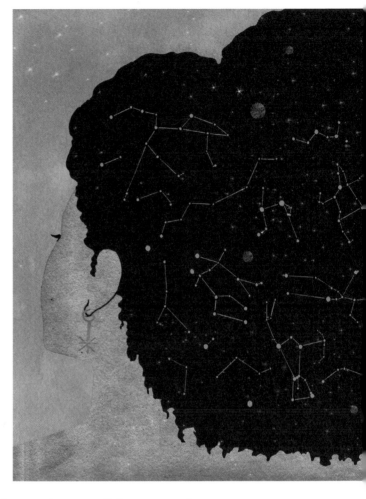

The next time you're feeling tiny, lonely, or undervalued, remember that we're all made up of the same chemical building blocks as stars. On a molecular level, you hold the world within you.

HOW TO KEEP IT GOING

Even if you live in a polluted city, you can still forge a meaningful relationship with the night sky. One of the quickest ways to do so is to simply draw what you see when you head out and look up. This will help you identify patterns that you can look into further. Like the moon and the sun, the consistency of these natural wonders will serve as a comfort.

THE FIRST FULL MOON OF WINTER

IT'S WRITING TIME

The first written words were immortalized in rock in the second millennium BC in an ancient language called Sumerian. Today, linguistics has blossomed into a 171,476-word (by some theories) repertoire in English alone.

We believe that a personal journal is the ultimate tool for self-exploration, and ideas aren't crystallized until they're immortalized on a page. Granted, as writers by trade we're biased, but research proves that writing can promote mental clarity, help us more efficiently navigate the world, and even cut down on our doctor visits.

Too often, the stories we tell ourselves aren't representative of the stories we experience. How many times have you panicked over an upcoming event—thinking up every terrible scenario—only to emerge on the other side unscathed? It's too easy to let your inner world call the shots without paying the outer one any mind. Journaling can help you break through negative thought patterns by transporting them onto the page, into the physical realm.

What makes pen and paper such a potent combo? Confronting the emotions that are bottled up inside may reduce physiological stress and the physical manifestations that come along with it. Pretty extraordinary for an activity we can do anytime, anywhere, for free.

A JOURNALING RITUAL FOR INTENTION

The full moon signals a moment of release, and journaling can help us let go of the past and move on from limiting beliefs. This ritual calls on the power of the written word to help us craft new stories.

WHAT YOU'LL NEED FROM THE OUTSIDE

* A journal, or just use the blank pages found in the beginning of this season
* A pen

WHAT YOU'LL NEED FROM WITHIN

＊ A willingness to be totally unfiltered and to write down anything and everything that comes to mind in the moment. Perfectionism has no place here.

INSTRUCTIONS

1. The night of a full moon, grab your journal and find a cozy place to nest. If you're able, sit so that the moon's light is shining down on you directly or through a window. If *la luna* isn't bright enough to see from where you're sitting, light a candle to evoke its energy.

2. Think back on the fall season, and make a list of all the words that come to mind. Write large, and give each word its own line on the page. Don't filter yourself or deem one thought too dark, too trite, too this, too that. Let your higher self do the talking. You'll know you're done when no new words come to mind.

3. Take a few moments to reflect on your list. Then, imagine doing the same exercise in the newness of spring, once winter has passed. What words do you want to see on the page? What do you hope to welcome into your life with this new season? With this same sense of limitless expression, write down these words. The imagination has been likened to an inner star, so let it shine some light on your goals and desires. Your musings can be vague or specific, universally desired or personal to you.

4. Looking back on your list, is there one word or phrase that sticks out to you? Again, leave story out of this and allow yourself to just gravitate. Once you've landed on a word, cut or tear it out of the journal, letting it become its own little fortune. Place it in a spot where you'll see it every day—whether it's on your bedroom mirror, in your wallet, or on your desk at work. Let it be a reminder of your commitment to grow and evolve this season.

HOW TO KEEP IT GOING

Keep the momentum of this ritual going by taking some time to write down something—*anything!*—every day. Recognize your notebook as so much more than a collection of lined pages. It's an opportunity to diagnose whatever's ailing you and concoct your own prescription. Every time you sit down to write, conduct a quick scan of your body and mind to see where you are in that moment. Know that whether you're feeling confused, overwhelmed, stressed, or elated, your journal can be a leveling tool.

* **STRESSED OUT?** Draw a line down the center of your page, labeling the column on the left "I feel worry because . . ." and the one on the right "But deep down I know . . ." Record your concerns, and then let your intuition start to diffuse them. Doing this one right before bed can be particularly helpful, as it primes the mind for uncluttered dreams.

* **ANTSY?** If you haven't yet immersed yourself in the lusty, multicolored vortex that is bullet journaling, we highly suggest you Google it right now. Bullet journals list menial tasks next to the ones that light us up inside. Next time you're feeling overwhelmed, write down all the tasks on your to-do list, then intersperse them with the ideas, people, or events that excite you.

* **DOWN ON YOURSELF?** Write down "Today I'm proud of myself for . . ." and let what comes next be a mix of your accomplishments, no matter how small they seem. We love doing this one on Sundays, and it reminds us that even a "lazy" day lounging around helps us conserve energy for the week ahead.

* **JOYOUS?** Immortalize that feeling with a detailed freewrite about the circumstances that led to this mood and how it made you feel deep in your bones. Or write yourself a cheer-up letter to read next time you're feeling down.

CHRISTMAS

♂ (DECEMBER 25)

LET YOUR ANGELS COME THROUGH

The idea that we all have angels and spirit guides is comforting but it can be difficult to completely get on board with. Nobody gets that more than Emma. While she never considered herself a skeptic per se, she was not a staunch believer in the afterlife and its tendency to subtly interact with us on Earth. That all changed when she had her first psychic reading.

When a renowned medium arrives in my office for a story about a new wave of mystic healers, I expect my experience to be relatively tame; maybe he'll have a few intuitive insights into my personality or be able to guess a deceased relative or two (none of them had particularly unique names, after all).

After a few seconds of sitting down in a room with me and shutting his eyes, the medium—an unassuming, not-at-all "woo-woo" figure—begins to list every departed member of my family's tree one by one as he feels their energy enter.

SEEING IS BELIEVING

So what *actually* makes a psychic a psychic? During a reading, they'll often use a combination of the four "clairs" (a French prefix that means light and bright) to see, hear, and feel someone's spiritual guides. So it's actually the guides who are doing the talking and predicting, while the psychic is just a highly in-tune conduit for their messages.

Clairvoyance: The ability to see spirits
Clairsentience: The ability to feel energy

Clairaudience: The ability to hear spirits speaking

Claircognizance: The ability to know things to be true that haven't happened yet

He speaks calmly of the practical jokes I used to play with my grandfather, who is saying how proud he is that I got into that "D" school (I had been accepted to Duke shortly after he passed away). He speaks of the necessity of my fairly recent breakup through the lens of my grandmother, who had always known he was bad news. He feels their energies and relays their messages with unrelenting accuracy and clarity. Then, he goes on to pick up on some of my energy, saying that I will eventually write a book (I landed this book deal a few weeks later) and move from New York City to someplace quieter (jury's still out on that one).

After telling friends of my experience the next day, I fielded a fair amount of "Of course he thinks you'll write a book—you're an editor" and "He could have just searched your name and found out how your grandpa died." Yes, he could have been making educated guesses, and yes, maybe he was just a Google wiz. But I choose to trust that the experience in that room on that day was something else: a reminder from the universe that there's so much more to this world than what we see and hear and touch.

It's comforting, in a way, this idea that we are never truly alone. That every time we step outside, we are surrounded not only by dozens of strangers but also by our loved ones who have left this physical plane but are still traveling with us on a separate one—touching us in ways that we can never explain or quantify but that we always somehow sense.

A CANDLE RITUAL FOR CONNECTION

The period just before the new year has always been one of celebration and familial togetherness. While winter celebrations such as Christmas, Kwanzaa, and Hanukkah are vastly different occasions, they all serve as opportunities for people to come together under one roof. Whichever one you're celebrating, we invite you to use it as an opportunity to connect to your loved ones—in this realm and beyond. And you don't need a visit from a celebrity medium to do it.

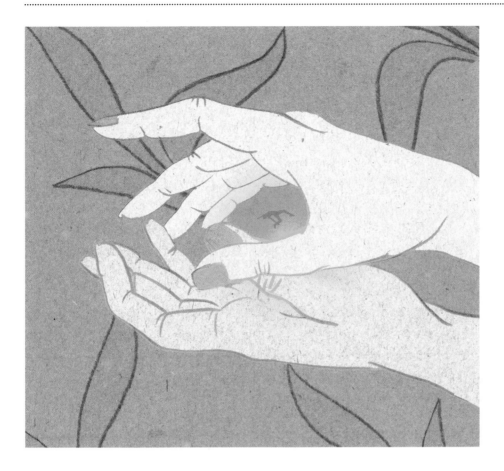

All it takes is a clear mind and a pinch of good faith. Ancient alchemists believed that fire housed the soul and ashes brought new life, so we'll be using candles to connect to the wisdom of the other world.

WHAT YOU'LL NEED FROM THE OUTSIDE

* Two candles: one purple, one white
* A crystal of your choice (refer to the crystals section of your toolbox on page 1)
* A photo of a family member or friend who has passed away
* Thieves essential oil, or another scent that reminds you of this time of year

WHAT YOU'LL NEED FROM WITHIN

✳ A quiet mind and relaxed body so you can hear and feel any subtle messages that come through

INSTRUCTIONS

1. Set aside a few moments one night during the holiday season to go into a room, turn off the lights, and set up a small altar display to a loved one who's passed. It could be as simple as a photo of them on a table or an arrangement of a few of their favorite belongings. It could be an extension of your existing altar if you're home or a new one if you're spending the holidays traveling to see family.

2. Light your white (the color of purity and peace) and purple (the color of spiritual connection and intuition) candles and place them on your altar. If you have your essential oils on hand, start diffusing these too to add another sensory element to the mix.

3. Watch the candle burn, hold the crystal in one hand, and take a few deep breaths to tune out the mental chatter. Think back to a time you shared with the person in question, allowing your mind to fill the scene with details and your body to feel a great sense of ease and peace at this memory. When you think you're done, keep going. Paint the scene in vivid color.

4. Repeat the mantra, either internally or aloud, "You are with me; you are always with me," for a few moments. Then, sit in silence and allow your body to feel the energy of their spirit in the room, attributing all sensation to his or her presence. Don't second-guess your feelings.

5. End the ceremony by blowing out your candle and holding the crystal over it. Imagine that the dance of the soft, smooth smoke holds the force of your guide and is charging your stone.

6. Place the crystal beside your tree, menorah, or another holiday display as a reminder of your spirit's presence. Know that they are with you through the occasion, watching in unseen but undying love.

HOW TO KEEP IT GOING

Tanya Carroll Richardson, a New York City–based author and psychic intuitive, knows a thing or two about channeling the spirit world. Here are a few of her top tips for harnessing your own intuition to pick up on the clues your guides are sending you throughout the year.

1. **KNOW THE LINGO.** The spiritual higher realm is a lot more complicated than you might think. We're all thought to be influenced by spirit guides (beings that once lived in this realm and now guide us from up above), angels (beings that have always existed in higher realms), and departed loved ones (such as grandparents who passed away when we were young and are often really active spiritual influences, since they've watched us grow up!). They all work together to guide us through life here on Earth, one clue or nudge at a time.

2. **SEE THE SIGNS.** Signs from the higher realm can be anything from a song, a sequence of numbers, an animal, or a gut feeling. Do you find yourself instinctively looking at the clock at the same time every day? Constantly hearing the same song on the radio? It could be because your guides get excited when you start to pick up on these clues and continue to send more.

3. **TRUST YOUR GUT.** Most of us are more intuitive (or clairsentient) than we think, so don't second-guess yourself. If you think you're receiving a sign from the universe, you probably are.

4. **PRACTICE MAKES PERFECT.** The more time you spend actively engaging with your guides, the better you'll get at it. One of Richardson's favorite suggestions for communicating with those in the other world? Write them a letter!

New Year's Eve

♂ (DECEMBER 31)

CRAFT YOUR OWN CALENDAR

December 31 doesn't have an especially colorful ancient history. In fact, the start of the new year wasn't always celebrated in winter; it used to fall on the spring equinox in March, which is also the start of the zodiac.

You see, our calendar used to correspond directly with the phases of the moon, but since the sky doesn't follow the exact same schedule year after year, it would often need to be corrected. It was Julius Caesar and a Greek astronomer named Sosigenes who created the basis of our modern calendar, but even their version didn't mark January 1 as the start of a new year. It wasn't until the calendar was again amended in the 1570s by Pope Gregory XIII that the day took on such significance.

Since the sixteenth century, we have dreamed up lofty New Year's Eve rituals to signify celebration and closure. While the sun sets on December 31 as it does any other day and rises on January 1 as it does on all the others, in between we now throw a welcome party for a new era—complete with fireworks, sparkles, and fresh, shiny resolutions. The fact that humans have assigned a day for such symbolism is a reminder of the ephemeral nature of time. Today is just another date that we imparted with meaning. In reality, any day could be a stage for new patterns to emerge.

AN ASTROLOGY RITUAL FOR ENCOURAGEMENT

While the reminder to set new resolutions is definitely invaluable, it shouldn't become restrictive. In other words, don't obsess over traditional, ego-driven New Year's plans of "lose X pounds" or "land X promotion." Instead, use the end of the calendar year as a time to reflect on all that you are and all that you want to be moving forward. There's no better moment to dive deeper into your natal chart (introduced on page 18) with a celebratory astrology ritual that illuminates all that we are carrying into the next phase.

WHAT YOU'LL NEED FROM THE OUTSIDE

* Your natal chart, which you can calculate online
* A journal, or just use the blank pages found in the beginning of this season
* A red pen
* A blue pen
* Colored pencils/art materials *(optional)*

WHAT YOU'LL NEED FROM WITHIN

* A willingness to step outside yourself and believe in the gifts the universe has already given you

INSTRUCTIONS

1. Enter the date, time, and location of your birth into a natal chart generator that also provides a written description of your chart (we recommend Cafe Astrology). If you're getting ready for a New Year's Eve party or celebration and are pressed for time, this can be done the day before. It's also a fun activity to do alongside a friend or relative if you want to make an event out of it!
2. Throw on your favorite song and begin to decode your chart, paying special attention to the zodiac signs of the aforementioned big three. Read through the descriptions of these signs, underlining the words and phrases that you want to bring into your life in the new year in blue and the ones you want to release in red.
3. Once you've completed your chart, transfer those words onto a fresh sheet of paper. Write the words you want to attract in larger font than

the ones you want to dispel. Think of it like a high-vibe decluttering, holding each word in a Marie Kondo–esque exploration. Does it bring you joy? If not, release it.

4. Grab any art supplies and create a true-to-you display of colors, patterns, and symbols that show what you want the new year to bring.

5. Look at this creation as a living, breathing vision board that you can add to as the year goes on. Store it near your altar so you can reference it whenever you need a reminder of the amazing qualities you inherently possess. Let these traits replace your typical list of resolutions. The universe has already placed all of them within you; they just need a little coaxing to surface.

HOW TO KEEP IT GOING

Jennifer Racioppi calls on astrology to empower female entrepreneurs to achieve their goals in business and beyond. She's an expert at reading natal charts in a purposeful, practical way. We asked for her top tips on how to glean tangible insights from your chart throughout the year, specifically when it comes to your career.

1. **LAY THE GROUNDWORK**. Locate your sun, your moon, and your rising sign, and understand how you relate to them (what house they're in, what planet rules them, and where the ruling planet is located). Then, look at the midheaven, which is on the cusp of the tenth house, at the very top of your chart. Any activity near the midheaven is crucial to your career, as it speaks to your social standing and reputation.

2. **GET IN YOUR ELEMENT**. Another important thing to consider when reading your chart for career is the breakdown of your elemental energies. Aries, Leo, and Sagittarius are fire signs; Capricorn, Taurus, and Virgo are earth signs; Gemini, Aquarius, and Libra are air signs; and Pisces, Cancer, and Scorpio are water signs. Think about the elemental makeup of your sun, moon, and rising signs. What elements do you have covered? Which ones are you lacking? Try welcoming in some of this missing energy with your routine. For instance, if your

chart is lacking fire, consider incorporating more warm, spicy food and aerobic activity into your day. Lacking air? Start a deep breathing or journaling routine. Balance your budget and get out into nature often if you need more grounded, earthly energy, and if you could use some more water in your life, spend your next night home watching a tearjerker movie or writing an emotion-fueled letter to a loved one.

3. DIG INTO YOUR SUN SIGN. Another point to consider is whether your sun sign is cardinal, mutable, or fixed, as this relates to your work style. Cardinal signs are the ones that kick off seasons (Capricorn, Aries, Cancer, and Libra), so when it comes to career, people with these sun signs are thought to be aggressive, assertive, and eager to initiate projects. Fixed signs (Aquarius, Taurus, Leo, and Scorpio) come after and hold down the middle of each season, making them stable and secure signs. The mutable signs (Gemini, Virgo, Sagittarius, and Pisces) appear at the end of the seasons, so they're the zodiac members who are flexible, go-with-the-flow types who prepare us for change.

4. DON'T FORGET THE HOUSES. Tenth (career success), second (self-worth), sixth (day-to-day routine), and eighth (payment from others) are commonly thought of as work and money houses, so pay close attention to those. Racioppi also refers to the third house (communication) and fifth house (creativity) often when she's counseling on career, so consider the aspects of your chart that fall into those too. For example, Emma's chatty, bubbly sun in Gemini falls into her tenth house of prestige and recognition, so it's no wonder she communicates through writing for a living.

ℭEW YEAR'S DAY

☌ (JANUARY 1)

A SMOKY SCIENCE

Smudging—the act of burning an herb and using its smoke to dispel negative energy—is an ancient practice that indigenous cultures have used in medicine, ritual, and religion for nearly two thousand years. The almighty smells of sage and sweetgrass have carried into today, and they're likely to greet you as soon as you walk into any mystical shop.

But smudging is about more than a nice aroma shrouded in historical significance. Smoke has been a vessel for medicine for millennia, used to treat everything from respiratory disease to toothaches. One comprehensive review found that at least fifty countries have harnessed the power of hundreds of herbs, most often as neurological remedies (think sedatives and hallucinogens) and pulmonary treatments (think decongestants) that were thought to work rapidly when inhaled through the nose. Recent studies validate this ancient method, and one found that an hour of burning wood and medicinal herbs caused a 94 percent reduction in atmospheric bacteria.

There is power in smoke beyond the medicinal. Traditional shamans and spiritual councils use dried sage to call upon ancestors and cleanse spirits. Any negativity or stress is thought to be absorbed by the smoke to then disappear into thin air.

There's now reason to believe that herbal smoke can in fact boost our mood too, by shifting the ionization of the air. If your memory of high school chemistry is hazy, ionization happens when atoms lose and gain electrons as they collide with other atoms or interact with light. Smoke from dried herbs is thought to make the ionic composition of the air more negative, and this negative ionization has been associated with improved memory and concentration and even lower rates of depression. In fact, herbs like ginseng, sage, and lemon balm are currently being explored as complementary treatments for Alzheimer's and dementia patients.

A HOME RITUAL FOR CLARITY

It's a new day, a new year, a new opportunity to lay the groundwork for growth. Yesterday, you did the inner work and identified the qualities you want to welcome into your life. Now, it's time to make the physical space to support them. With this ritual, you'll harness the cleansing, brain-boosting power of herbs to kick off the year with clarity of mind.

WHAT YOU'LL NEED FROM THE OUTSIDE

* Dried herbs of your choosing (we love sage and lavender)
* A large seashell or a plate or bowl

WHAT YOU'LL NEED FROM WITHIN

* A vision of all the energy you want to welcome into your life this year, so you can design your space to support it

INSTRUCTIONS

1. Prepare your home by opening all doors and windows to get a nice airflow going. (If it's too cold, crack one open symbolically.)
2. Light the end of your herbal bundle, and let it burn for a few seconds before blowing it out. Set it down in your seashell, letting the smoke fade softly into the air. The seashell represents the water element, the flame represents fire, the breath to blow it out represents air, and the herbs themselves represent earth.
3. Wave the smoky stick around you, starting it above your head and moving down your body slowly. As you bathe yourself in the smoke, feel it absorbing any internal negativity and leaving behind only light. Wave the stick in a figure-eight pattern to lock in this energy. The

symbol that represents infinity and is mirrored in our DNA is believed to be deeply healing.

4. Now that you have cleansed yourself, it's time to tackle the rest of your space. As you walk room to room, wave your sage stick slowly—up to the ceiling, down to the floor, and into tight corners. Let your intuition tell you which spots need a little bit more cleansing. You can also let feng shui properties guide your path (more on that in the next section). Make the entire process a moving meditation by repeating the mantra "I graciously accept the positive and graciously let go of the negative."

5. Bring the ritual to a close by rubbing the smudge stick into your shell to extinguish its smoke. Sprinkle any resulting ashes outside to return them to the earth. Know you can repeat this ritual anytime your home feels stale or uninspired.

HOW TO KEEP IT GOING

Now that you've cleared the negativity out of your space, it's time to start filling it with good vibes. Calling on feng shui—the ancient Chinese practice of arranging surroundings to promote the flow of positive energy—adds another layer to your home cleanse. Feng shui splits the home into nine areas, creating what's known as a *bagua* map. Each section of the perimeter is called a *gua*, and the center of your home is always the ninth component.

1	2	3
4	5	6
7	8	9

Check out what each *gua* represents and think about which ones you want to accentuate with the energetic enhancements that architect and feng shui master Anjie Cho recommends. If tackling your whole house feels too daunting, start small by dividing your bedroom, or even your desk, into these areas.

1. **WEALTH**. Place a piece of natural citrine, which is thought to attract prosperity, in the abundance area of your home.
2. **RECOGNITION AND FAME**. A living green plant (or in multiples of three, five, or nine) provides abundant qi, the unbounded inspiration necessary for growth.
3. **MARRIAGE**. A pair of tumbled rose quartz can ignite the relationship area of the bedroom with loving energy, as well as nurture self-love and gentleness. If you're standing in the doorway to your bedroom looking into the center of the room, it's the far-right corner.
4. **FAMILY AND NEW BEGINNINGS**. Hang a charm for each of the Chinese zodiac animals on a single string. Each one represents a different archetype and personality, so binding them by a thread symbolizes familial harmony.
5. **HEALTH**. The health area is located in the center, or heart, of your home. It relates to the earth and grounding, so place muted, earthy tones throughout.
6. **COMPLETION AND CHILDREN**. A metal wind chime with five cylinders (to represent the five elements) sends a reverberating song that signifies loving completion through your entire space.
7. **KNOWLEDGE AND SELF-CULTIVATION**. Use paint or accessories to fill this area with deep, dark blues that can elicit knowledge, skillfulness, and spirituality.
8. **CAREER**. Splurge on a small fountain or fish tank to evoke the water element associated with career success and new opportunities.
9. **BENEFACTORS AND TRAVEL**. If you're looking to travel more, consider getting a metal pinwheel to symbolize the winds of change and opportunity for boundless exploration.

VALENTINE'S DAY

𝄞 (FEBRUARY 14)

BREWING A LOVE POTION

February 14 hasn't always been defined by chocolates and heart-eye emojis. Our modern celebrations grew from a rich history dating all the way back to the love spells of ancient Greece.

Greeks gathered at stately sanctuaries, each one dedicated to a certain god, in the hopes of receiving some of that deity's guidance. Every temple was unique and built to evoke the nature of its associated spirit, with the temple of Poseidon, the god of the sea, showcasing a spectacular view of the water. The temple of Aphrodite, the goddess of love, passion, and fertility, was rife with women hoping to become pregnant, get married, or refuel an existing relationship. Armed with honey cakes, flowers, and sweet fruits as their currency, they sang hymns and made offerings to Aphrodite, pouring water on the earth to seal their intentions.

Professions of love have taken on different forms since these early days, but flowers are a theme in most of them. Through the years, we've even assigned identities and personas to petals and formed a romantic language of flowers.

FLOWER POWER

Flowers were once referred to as "messengers of the heart," relics from nature that could silently speak volumes. Early evidence of the language of flowers, or floriography, lies in a note from Walahfrid Strabo, a monk who lived in the 800s. When writing about his monastery garden, he referenced two of the earliest plants imbued with meaning: the rose, a symbol of "the spilt blood of the martyrs," and the lily, a "shining symbol of faith." The rose, he said, was plucked for war, the lily for peace.

This hidden language continued to develop in the Middle Ages. One story from the time spoke of lovers who were not able to be together, so they started sending each other tear-stained roses as symbols of passion and pain.

The messages in flowers really started to bloom in tight-lipped Victorian England, when certain words were too taboo to speak aloud. Bouquets became letters of sorts, passed along between people to express joy, love, and hatred. Around that time, a whole host of new flowers made their way to Europe from the Americas, enough to keep curious decoders very busy. Equipped with flower dictionaries, people could spend days interpreting the flowers they received from friends, family, and love interests, searching for meaning in the shape and color of every petal. Unsurprisingly, this left a lot of room for misinterpretation, and the language largely fell out of style by the twentieth century.

You can still hear some whispers of the language of flowers today. Most of us know that a red rose symbolizes love and passion, while a sunflower is all about friendship, longevity, and warmth.

A FLORAL FACIAL STEAM FOR FEMININITY AND SELF-LOVE

Everyone can use today's holiday to celebrate the warm and fuzzies that find us as we navigate life, whether or not we have a partner. This ritual calls on flowers—which can serve as powerful reminders of light, even in the depths of winter—to express radical self-love.

WHAT YOU'LL NEED FROM THE OUTSIDE

* Rosemary (flower or essential oil)
* Lavender (flower or essential oil)
* An iris or a fresh flower of your choosing if irises are not available in your area

* A large bowl of boiling water
* A towel

WHAT YOU'LL NEED FROM WITHIN

* A few deep breaths
* A vision of the type of love and passion you're seeking

INSTRUCTIONS

1. Pour a pot of boiling water into a bowl until it's about halfway full. Quickly add five sprigs of fresh rosemary or five drops of rosemary oil to symbolize remembrance of the past and enduring love for the future. Add five sprigs of fresh lavender or five drops of lavender oil to symbolize femininity and spirituality. Last, throw an iris, symbolizing hope and light, into the fragrant, colorful mix, reserving one of its petals for later.

2. Lean over so your face sits just above the water line, and then drape a towel over your head to encapsulate the steam. Take in the bowl's messages of past, present, and future by reflecting on past loves (romantic or otherwise), appreciating present ones, and visualizing loves of the future.

3. Let the flowers, with their dance through the seasons, blooming, growing, dying, and blooming again, remind you that love is far from static. Love peaks and dips through time, but it never becomes any less beautiful. Sit for five to ten minutes, wrapped in the warmth, infusing yourself in this unconditional, unwavering love with every inhale.

4. Arise from the steam once the water has cooled down, and hold your hands to your face so they can encapsulate this energy. Then, grab the single petal you have left over, closing it in your palms and charging it with the intention of endless love through winter.

HOW TO KEEP IT GOING

According to the language of flowers, each of the following holds a deeply loving energy of its own. Moving forward, you can continue to use these in facial steams, drop some of their petals in a bath, craft them into a flower essence, or simply get into the habit of gifting yourself a fresh bouquet each week.

* Hibiscus: fragile beauty
* Passionflower: faith and affection
* Pink rose: happiness and connection
* Primrose: young love
* Red rose: passion and desire
* Sunflower: warmth and prosperity
* Tulip: imagination and dreaminess
* White carnation: good luck
* White rose: charm and innocence

TELL A FAIRY TALE DAY

✿ (FEBRUARY 26)

HAPPILY EVER AFTER, ALWAYS

With roots in the Latin word *fatum*, or "to enchant," and the French word *feerie*, or "illusion," fairy tales imbue traditional storytelling with an extra dose of imagination. They resemble the myths and fables passed through generations since the beginning of time, but add character, plot, and a hearty dose of fantasy to the mix. They transport us to a land of once upon a time, a place where make-believe and reality can intermingle to weave a happily ever after. As one anonymous philosopher put it long ago, "the fairy tale is a poetic presentation of a spiritual truth."

Before the advent of the printing press, these stories were recited orally, adopting new personalities with each telling. Anthropologists have traced the stories of Little Red Riding Hood to upward of 58 versions and Rapunzel to 310 different tellings across time and culture. Some of the first books that married text and illustrations were *Twinkle, Twinkle Little Star* and *Dance Little Baby, Dance Up High.*

As our stories have evolved, so too have the mythical fairies that inhabit them. Victorian-era fairies took on a more humble, human form than the cloaked, wanded fairy godmothers we're now used to. They were beautiful women in long, loose dresses, often crowned with the flowers and butterflies of the forests they called home. They at once epitomized femininity and rebellion, forgoing more traditional paths to live among nature.

Fairies have always been spirit incarnated. They epitomize a way of living that is wild and uninhibited, mysterious and certainly magical.

A DRAWING RITUAL FOR REBIRTH

Whether you left your windows open so Peter Pan and Tink could whisk you off to Neverland or dubbed yourself Sleeping Beauty and fought off the evil curse, most of us have childhood memories colored by fairy tales. Though its exact origins are unknown, Tell a Fairy Tale Day serves as an occasion to remember our youth—a time when mystical lands didn't feel so far away after all. Today, let's step forward as people who carry our own magic, the enchanted protagonists of our own stories.

WHAT YOU'LL NEED FROM THE OUTSIDE

* A piece of blank paper
* Two different colored pens, preferably one black and one blue or red

WHAT YOU'LL NEED FROM WITHIN

* A willingness to paint your own picture, even if you're "not an artist"

INSTRUCTIONS

1. Put on a song that you associate with a difficult time in your life that you have worked through. It could be the anthem of a past relationship or a melody that was the backdrop to a loss. Close your eyes, and imagine the person you were during this time, steadily breathing through the song's chorus and refrain until you reach the end of the tune.
2. Holding on to this image, take your black or darker pen and sketch the person you saw. It doesn't need to be an accurate portrayal of you. It doesn't even need to take a human form. Let the visualization you just completed guide your hand without judgment.
3. Now, put on a song that you love and that brings a smile to your face. Close your eyes, and see both the being you are in this moment and

the one you wish to someday become. What does she look like dancing in the noise?

4. Sketch out this figure in the lighter color, again letting your imagination dictate the lines on the page. Hold on to this person, and use her as a bookmark to keep in your books moving forward, if you wish.

HOW TO KEEP IT GOING

Even if you don't consider yourself particularly artsy, chances are you could benefit from taking a few minutes to get creative every once in a while. Playing in the visual arts arena is a way to tap into a meditative flow state while letting out some of your inner dialogue. Here are a few ways to harness the five senses to make art an even more mindful experience.

* **HEAR**. Throw on a song and let the notes guide your pen or brush. Think of it as a chance to let your senses mingle and inform one another, even if you don't make it past the end of the tune.
* **TOUCH**. Take a pencil and walk around your house, local park, or favorite café (though you might want to check with the owner first), stopping at any texture that speaks to the space—be it a table, book, or plant. Then, place your paper over them and rub your pencil so the texture bleeds onto the page. Let these etchings be the base of the creation, taking the portrait wherever you wish from there.
* **SIGHT**. Choose an object that you really *don't* like—maybe it's the antique table your partner insists you keep in the house or the filing system that reminds you of tax season. Sketch it out in detail. By translating it to the page, you're separating its physical form and the emotions you attach to it and reminding yourself that, at the end of the day, it's just another thing.
* **TASTE**. The next time you're eating a solo meal—or looking to do something a little different with your dining buddy—bring your pen and pencil to the table. Eat slowly and mindfully, closing your eyes with each bite to really appreciate the flavor and texture. Then, make a fun little rendition of how the taste would translate to a physical

object that isn't food. Would your salad be a grouchy old man? Your pasta a luxuriously made bed?

* **SMELL**. Get into the routine of diffusing an essential oil in your bedroom every night, choosing a color that best suits it before you go to sleep. Before long, you'll have a little aromatic calendar of your own.

International Women's Day

σ (MARCH 8)

THE SONG OF SISTERHOOD

Following an invite from two of her favorite spiritual teachers, Alexandra Roxo and Ruby Warrington, the cocreators of Moon Club, Emma signed on to a three-day women's gathering upstate to celebrate the Leo new moon. She had no idea what she was in for. . . .

I am sitting cross-legged in a room, surrounded by twenty women, about a quarter of whose names I know. We're less than a day into a new-moon retreat in upstate New York, though I use the word "retreat" lightly since the time we've spent together in this cabin in the woods feels infinitely more demanding, draining, and intense than any work I did Monday through Friday. In an ode to the darkness that's enveloping the sky outside, we strangers are using this weekend as an opportunity to dive into our shadow side—that messy, gritty, raw, emotional part of ourselves that isn't often invited out.

Our fearless leaders tell us to completely shed our masks with this next exercise. They invite us to sit across from a partner and look into her left eye. Then, they tell us to scream and wail and moan at this woman, feeling safe in the knowledge that she's holding space for our release, that she won't break the gaze no matter how wild things get.

My partner and I don't know anything about each other besides the fact that we're both women in this world. And somehow, that's enough. We un-flinchingly hold each other's eyes in a show of support and understanding. It's with the silent promise she makes that I let my voice join the chorus.

The sound is enormous—the years of frustration and sadness and anger and relief fuse together in a song of rebellion and strength. We release honestly, revolt wholly. After silencing some of our emotions for so long—shutting them out for the sake of others or our own inner critics—the act of letting go like nobody is watching is beyond cathartic. The results are somehow beautiful in their rawness; the symphony of feminine power is a strangely melodic one.

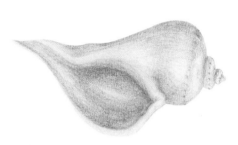

Later that night we conduct a ritual to carry these emotions into the physical world, where they can ultimately be released. Each one of us throws something that's holding us back into the fire, letting it drift up with the smoke and dissipate into the crisp night air. I let go of self-consciousness and self-sabotage. I release the need to feel validated by anyone but myself. *We speak these words not just for ourselves but for everyone else in the circle. To step out of our brains and feel into our bellies, where that wild feminine soul lives, in an act of animalistic release.*

That night, we weren't divided by our different stories but united in the shared experience of womanhood. How incredible it is, to think of ourselves as a collective. To simultaneously drop our shadows so we can shine a little brighter out in the world together.

A PARTNER RITUAL FOR STABILITY

Let's join together for International Women's Day to scream, not whisper, our worth. The holiday got its start in the labor movements of the twentieth century in North America and Europe, marking a pivotal turn in the women's rights movement. Now endorsed by the United Nations, it's a reminder to celebrate the power and potential that we women were forced to hide for so long. This last spirit holiday of the season signals a moment to look into the future and see how you can carry this strength forward.

WHAT YOU'LL NEED FROM THE OUTSIDE

* A friend
* A crystal or other special (small) object for each of you
* A pen and a journal for each of you

* The capacity to hold space for another, and the trust that helping another shine brighter doesn't dim your own flame

INSTRUCTIONS

1. Grab your friend and find a comfy, open place on the floor to sit. Take off your shoes and, facing each other, come to a seat.
2. Envision something you'd like to manifest this spring, and have your friend do the same. Take your time with this. Get as specific as you can: If you want a raise, write down your goal salary. If you want a promotion, what would your new title and role be? If you want to find love, what qualities are important to you in a mate? If it helps, write it down.
3. Once you've both finished, speak your vision aloud to your friend. Make it a point to hold eye contact with each other as you're talking, and don't break it. The act of simply giving your goal a voice—letting it live outside your mind, no matter how silly it feels—is extremely powerful. Each person gets a turn.
4. When you're done, turn away from each other and sit back-to-back with your legs bent or extended, whatever is comfortable. Take a moment to make sure you feel secure in your own foundation.
5. In silence, envision your friend meeting the goal she told you about so passionately. What would it look like were she to achieve it? What will it take for her to get there from where she is? Being generous with your energy, give her what she needs. Trust that holding space for others to shine doesn't dim your own light.
6. At the same time, feel her energy. Feel her back on yours, and feel supported in your endeavors. Stay here for as long as you wish.
7. After you're finished, write down any downloads, observations, and feelings that came up. Share as long as you are comfortable doing so.

You can expand on this by gathering in a women's circle or hosting your own. The reality is that many of our trials and tribulations, even the most difficult ones, are part of the human journey even though it feels as though you're facing them alone most of the time. Chances are someone else has shared a similar experience or can relate to yours. When we don't feel alone, the burden of our problems is shared and less heavy. Whether you share openly or choose to simply receive, you will leave the circle with new insights, different perspectives, and a deeper sense of gratitude.

HOW TO KEEP IT GOING

Hosting a women's circle is different from simply catching up with friends because it comes with ground rules, lends new perspectives, and allows you to be your truest self. There are no strings attached, no feelings to be hurt, and no expectations to live up to. Setting boundaries is the key to a successful circle. Here are some pointers from Paula Mallis, the founder of WMN Space in Los Angeles and a facilitator of hundreds of women's circles.

1. **YOU DON'T NEED AN ALTAR**. So many of the circles at WMN Space have been about not creating an altar. An altar is a physical representation of the circle coming together, but in so much of the experience of the circle, it doesn't matter if the altar is there. An altar is a beautiful offering. We can have the oils. We can have the altar. But those physical manifestations of how we start to create the circle to sit in are not entirely necessary.

2. **CLEAR THE SPACE**. It is important to intentionally clear the space, whether you feel called to hold circle in your home, rent a space, or do it outside. Before everyone arrives, clear the space with sage or palo santo. Upon sitting down in circle, cue everyone to return to the present moment—ask them to leave their to-do lists, the day up until this moment, and their troubles at the door. If there is anything within the circle, the space, or ourselves that doesn't serve, we let it go.

3. **CHOOSE AN INTENTION.** To set an intention is to answer the question: Why do we come to circle? What you'll find is that many women have similar intentions—community and connection are the ones that come up most often. Your intention can be anything that resonates with where you are, as long as it's broad enough to encompass everyone's experience. Some ideas to get you started include transitions, loss, strength, and unblocking creativity. Setting an intention also helps to keep a group focused—otherwise it's easy to go off topic. When an intention is set, it's simple to refocus. The intention also helps the facilitator hold space. How you hold space for women who want to conceive is different from how you hold space for women who are pregnant, for example.

4. **SET GROUND RULES.** In addition to setting clear intentions, it's important to set ground rules. Here are a few examples:
   * **DON'T APOLOGIZE FOR CRYING.** Too often it's our default to utter an apology after getting emotional, but crying in circle is encouraged. Holding space for it honors where someone is in that moment. Crying is a release that can lead to insights and a feeling of being cleansed, and sometimes help the sadness, frustration, or anger move.
   * **NO CROSS TALK.** This is a simple way of ensuring that anyone who shares is not cut off or invalidated. It helps women feel safe and heard.
   * **ASK WOMEN TO LISTEN FROM A HEART-CENTERED PLACE, AND WITH NEUTRALITY.** Listening without judgment to your own thoughts or those of the women sharing gives people the dignity of their own process. Everyone is on a journey. Listening without judgment is a practice of going back to love, which allows us to be neutral.

5. **LET COMMUNITY HAPPEN.** These days, women want to work together, create together, and mother together more, and women's circles are helping them work through their processes. The key is to let go of the

need to guide and solve and pursue. Simply allowing for connections, or even calling them in, is a way to let community happen. Don't resist it.

6. **TRY TO TIME IT WITH A NEW OR FULL MOON.** It is really powerful to gather during a new or full moon. The moon and the sun are our guides. To align ourselves with those energies creates a palpable power for gathering.

ᵴPRING

Behold, my friends, the spring is come; the earth has gladly
received the embraces of the sun, and we shall soon
see the results of their love.

—SITTING BULL

A T THE START OF SPRING, the weather likely still feels like winter. According to the common adage, March is supposed to go in like a lion and out like a lamb, but spring rarely arrives without a bite. It takes a moment to warm up, and often, so do we.

But when it does, it's a welcome sign of renewal, rebirth, and starting fresh. Harnessing the clearing energy of spring is paramount near or on the equinox. It's prime time to purge unnecessary things from your home, workspace, inbox, even your social media accounts, to make room for what the season can bring. The spring equinox, like the autumnal equinox, is a time of transition—it's so important to stay grounded, to sync with the season, and to know that brighter, warmer days lie ahead.

ᵴPRING: A HISTORY

In many historic cultures, springtime coincided with the new year. In Persia, around 500 AD, citizens praised their leader with opulence: gifts, poetry, flamboyant attire, street performances, and, most of all, roses. Called

Nowruz today, the vernal equinox is still celebrated by Iranians today as their new year, but with activities far less showy than they used to be.

In ancient Greek mythology, the goddess Demeter ruled the earth's fertility and harvest. As the story goes, her daughter, Persephone, was abducted by Hades and taken to the underworld. While Demeter searched endlessly for her daughter, the plants on Earth began to wither and die. One day, when Demeter finally found Persephone, Hades swore he'd release her only if she hadn't eaten anything during her stay in the underworld. Unfortunately, Persephone had eaten six pomegranate seeds, which bound her to the underworld for six months of every year. It was not Persephone's absence that spurred the bleak months of late autumn and early winter—it was Demeter's sadness borne from her missing daughter that made the earth wilt until spring, when she would return. As heartbreaking as that is, the inverse is also true: When Persephone returns to the heavens, harvest goddess Demeter's spirits lift and bring the vegetation with them. Persephone is often depicted holding grains, a sign of fertility, growth, and potential.

In medieval times, people saw the coming of spring as a sign to celebrate the return of longer days, warmer weather, and love. Maypoles, games, and warm-weather festivals were ways to meet your mate.

People travel near and far to embrace the rays of special springtime sunshine on top of ancient Mesoamerican city Teotihuacán's Pyramid of the Sun. Many travelers believe that wearing all white amplifies the effects of the spring sunshine. Like the beginning of spring, the pyramid is a fertility symbol.

As such, spring is a time to experience renewed togetherness—throughout history, you'll see across varying cultures that the message is more or less the same. People were grateful for winter to pass and for the potential to begin again.

Nature of the Season

According to Traditional Chinese Medicine (TCM) and Ayurveda, spring is prime time for a cleanse. We're not suggesting you go on a juice cleanse, but eliminating unwanted sugar and other refined foods from your diet and focusing on whole, home-cooked foods can do a body good. The organs associated with spring according to TCM are liver and gallbladder, both responsible for removing toxins from our bodies. Supporting these organs with greens, wheatgrass, sprouts, and herbs such as dandelion, peppermint, and nettle will keep you feeling light and buoyant throughout the season, shaking off the doldrums and heaviness of winter. Ayurveda calls for oleation—the use of oil internally as ghee (clarified butter) and externally as moisturizer, a practice called abhyanga. Using both in tandem is said to soften hard toxins and help flush them out of the body.

While the ground is thawing, resilient crocuses are one of the first flowers to sprout. An explosion of cherry blossoms usually coincides with the first few weeks of spring, followed by other tree flowers that eventually give way to new leaves and greenery. Their blooming is a sign to start planting other seeds and flowers. Spring is a great time to add plants to your home, to start a garden, and, of course, to get started on a purge of all things that don't serve you—from your home base, to work, to personal relationships, to habits.

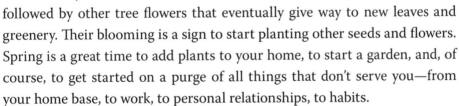

Modern Spring Ritual

Modern spring rituals around Easter and Passover are based on growth and renewal. In Christianity, Easter commemorates the day Jesus rose from the dead; on Passover, Jews fast and then feast as they celebrate freedom from

Egyptian slavery. While they're both deeply meaningful and demanding of those who celebrate, they end in a jovial feast or a sigh of relief when normal routines resume.

In the spring, we may find ourselves with excess energy to burn as we move past the slowness of winter and begin to release anything that was holding us down. In schools, spring marks the homestretch before summer vacation; in work, we bring renewed passion to our projects; and at home, we begin to rearrange, cleanse, and spend more time outside as we embrace the transition.

SPRING IS A TIME TO . . .

* Clean your personal, work, and shared spaces, getting rid of anything you don't need and making room for newness.
* Draw up a plan for pursuing your intentions, nurturing them like seedlings.
* Start breaking a sweat—bonus points if you take it outside.
* Add more fresh fruits and cleansing greens to your diet.
* Ignite new creative projects.
* Collaborate with others instead of turning inward.

THE SPRING EQUINOX

START FRESH

One of the most interesting vernal equinox celebrations, known as Shunbun no Hi, comes from Japan. There, the equinox was a time for families to visit and clean the graves of loved ones, as well as their own homes, because Buddhist beliefs maintain that communication with the spirit realm increases when day and night are equal lengths. Some still do this, but it's also become a nationwide holiday off from work and school for people to celebrate the coming of spring and blooming *hanami*—the explosion of cherry blossoms—with their families.

In the United States and China, some people have been known to try to balance eggs vertically on flat surfaces today, inspired by the notion that the earth has a unique angle and gravitational pull on the equinox. While this is a myth, the egg is a bona fide symbol of spring in many holidays, especially on Easter and on the seder plate in Passover.

A SALT BATH RITUAL FOR CLEANSING

To prepare for a season of growth, it's important to move past the doldrums of winter. This cleansing bath ritual will purify your body through one of your biggest organs—your skin—washing away worries and making space for new beginnings this spring.

WHAT YOU'LL NEED FROM THE OUTSIDE

* A tub
* A twenty-minute playlist
* Magnesium-enriched bath salts
* Lavender and tea tree essential oils *(optional)*
* Body oil

WHAT YOU'LL NEED FROM WITHIN

∗ The desire to reflect and let go

INSTRUCTIONS

1. Once your bath is full, drop one to two cups of magnesium-enriched salts in it (depending on how big your tub is). Then, add a few drops of lavender and one to two drops of tea tree essential oils, if you want a smell-good element. Tea tree is an excellent scent to bridge spring and winter. It's icy and associated with winter's cold temperature, but it's also very refreshing, focusing, and astringent. Paired with lavender, it's a reminder to be both relaxed and awake, embracing the transition from winter to spring.

2. Allow your twenty-minute playlist to be your timer, and leave your tech out of reach.

3. As soon as you're settled in the water, allow your eyes to close. If you suspect you might fall asleep, maintain a soft gaze instead.

4. While you're in the bath, know that the salt is working to cleanse you from the outside in due to its high magnesium content, a mineral that's essential in helping tight and sore muscles to release. Envision three things you can let go of this spring. What would happen if you released them? They can be material things, negative self-talk, or relationships that no longer serve you. Be honest.

5. Find where they are in your body. Do you hold that relationship as tension around your heart? Breathe into it. Or perhaps you keep your late-night hours in your shoulders. Send them love. Do this for each release.

6. If you're comfortable, stay in the water until your playlist ends. Dry off, leaving your skin a little damp, and nourish your body with a good body oil. Relax as you take it easy. Feel free to write about your experience afterward.

If you don't have access to a tub, you can do this in the shower. Drip a few drops of essential oils in the shower both near the drain and at the other end of the tub—try to avoid the area where you stand because they can be slippery! Before you lather up and after you're rinsed off, take the magnesium salts and apply them to your skin as you would a scrub, without rubbing too hard. Stay there for a few minutes with the salt on your skin and the steam building in the shower. Feel free to shave, wash your hair, and go about your normal shower routine with the salts on. Or, after three to five minutes of relaxing, rinse and proceed as usual.

HOW TO KEEP IT GOING

Britta Plug, a holistic aesthetician and health coach based in Brooklyn, New York, performs and teaches a gentle lymphatic drainage massage to clients based on the ancient technique of gua sha. *Here she advises on how to add detoxifying, lymph-moving practices to your bathing ritual. Try them out the next time you get out of the bath.*

1. Dry brushing stimulates lymphatic flow for internal detoxification and will begin to slough dead winter skin cells. Use a brush with some copper bristles. Start at the farthest point from the heart—your feet and ankles—and work up your legs, followed by your arms, and then your tummy.
2. On your limbs, perform long, light, and brisk strokes up toward the heart. Repeat each stroke a few times.
3. Over your joints, do small, light circles.
4. On your abdomen, follow the path of your colon for maximum detox: from your right hip point, brush up to the bottom of your rib cage to mimic your ascending colon. Next, brush along the top of your abdomen, the bottom of your rib cage, from the right side to the left, to follow your transverse colon. Finally, brush down the left side from your bottom rib to hip point for your descending colon.

5. Your back is harder to get to, but it's nice to make strokes outward over the backs of your shoulders. Support your working arm at the elbow with your nonworking hand, like a triceps stretch. This movement flushes toward the lymph nodes at your armpit. Finally, a few strokes downward and outward on your lower back, flushing in the general direction of your hips.

6. Skip your breasts unless you have an extra-soft bristle brush. Your neck and face are also too delicate for a body brush.

Spring is prime allergy season, and sinus issues can cause stagnation and inflammation in your face, as well as puffy eyes. After you dry brush your body, use this facial self-massage technique to manipulate the fascia—the layer of connective tissue right under the skin—and help relieve sinus pressure and discomfort from allergies. Hold each point for three deep breaths in and out.

* Inner corners of eyebrows, pressing up on the brow bone
* Outer corners of eyes
* Right outside the nostrils
* Under the apples of your cheekbones, pressing upward on the bone

THE FIRST NEW MOON OF SPRING

OPEN SESAME

Anyone who lives near a tidal body of water has felt the effects of the moon. During a full or new moon, its gravitational pull is strongest, pulling high tides higher and pushing low tides lower. The human body is mostly made of water (70 percent, according to NASA), so logic would dictate that the moon has an effect on us too. As believers in the power of ritual, moving with this energy and not resisting it—even if that feels counter to what you want or think you want—is key to gaining insights, moving past blocks, and learning more about yourself.

A new-moon sky is an inky backdrop to little pearls, and in springtime they're reminiscent of beads of morning dew—a sign of warming from within and invigoration. If winter reminded us to look up at the stars and then within ourselves, then spring is a look forward. The clocks spring forward, the days get longer, and the earth responds by awakening. This crescendo of yang energy when combined with congruent energetics of the yin new moon create fertile ground for preparation, release, and growth.

Yoga—which technically means the union of mind and body, or body and breath—is always a clearing practice. Moving the body in all directions opens you up as a vessel to receive. As the founder of Katonah yoga and registered massage therapist (and one of Lindsay's teachers) Nevine Michaan says, the body is not a temple; it's a house. You live in a house, you can make a mess in the house, you can even have a party in the house—but you have to clean it up and clean it out. Yoga is a purification of the body so we can access our mind from a calm, quiet place.

A MOONLIT YOGA RITUAL FOR GROWTH

This yoga sequence will start with grounding poses that make a lot of contact with the earth and end in a seed to mimic the phases of the moon.

WHAT YOU'LL NEED FROM THE OUTSIDE

* A yoga mat
* A clear window—no shades or curtains
* Palo santo sticks *(optional)*

WHAT YOU'LL NEED FROM WITHIN

* A desire to shed old layers

INSTRUCTIONS

1. Before beginning the moon salutation, set up your mat in a spot that faces a window, preferably one where you can see the moon. Burn your palo santo if desired—it's a clearing scent.
2. Follow this sequence of poses:

   HERO'S POSE. Start in a hero's pose, sitting on your shins, with your hands in a prayer position. Inhale, and sweep your arms up overhead.

CHILD'S POSE. Exhale and bow forward into a child's pose, draping your body over your thighs and stretching your arms away from your ears, out in front of you

RIGHT SIDE STRETCH. Crawl your hands over to the left, expanding the right-side waist. Extend your right hand as far forward and right as it will go while anchoring down with your left hip. Take a few belly breaths here, as your body mimics the shape of a crescent moon. Come back to center.

LEFT SIDE STRETCH. Crawl your hands over to the right, expanding the left-side waist. Extend your left hand as far forward and left as it will go while anchoring down with your right hip. Take a few belly breaths here, as your body mimics the shape of a crescent moon. Come back to center.

SEED POSE. Exhale, and, in child's pose, grab your feet with your hands, connecting to the earth

HERO'S POSE. Inhaling slowly, come back to sit by rolling up, one vertebra at a time. Exhale and bring your hands to your heart to seal the practice. Repeat this flow as many times as you like.

HOW TO KEEP IT GOING

Kumi Sawyers, a yoga teacher, massage therapist, and Ayurveda expert, shares tips on how to prepare your space for a home yoga practice with springtime in mind.

Making your home a sacred place takes work. And spring, being the season of cleansing and renewal, is the perfect time to do it. On the first warm days, it's normal to feel the urge to open the windows and move the stale energy of winter out, inviting in spring's winds of change. It's the time to put away heavy winter wools and replace them with light summer cottons. Following suit, we switch out our boots for sandals and strip the down comforters off our beds. We do this every year when the seasons change. Taking these seemingly mundane chores and turning them into rituals imbued with intention and purpose is the secret ingredient to making your home sacred. Here's a little spring cleaning for the soul:

1. Start by putting on music that gets you moving and inspires you.

2. Our homes—our external environments—are direct reflections of our internal environment, so we must first begin by cleaning up within. Start by taking a good look at your life. See where you are and know where you want to go. Set a guiding intention—not a goal, but a guideline that will help you reach your goals. Gather the tools from your metaphorical toolkit that will help you abide, and let go of the things that are distracting. Spring is the time for change; let it happen.

3. Next, declutter. Go through your closets and drawers. Get rid of any old papers, clothes, appliances, and anything else that no longer serves a purpose. Bonus points if you donate them. All of your belongings should have a place to fit comfortably inside your home, the same way your thoughts and feelings fit comfortably inside you.

4. Create a cleansing water with essential oils of lemon (a natural antibacterial and antiseptic) and cedar (a wood, which is the element associated with spring) to use for wiping down surfaces and mopping your floors.

5. Open the windows to aerate your space.

6. Take this as an opportunity to connect with your home. Make contact with your belongings and remember the stories they have to tell. This will help to breathe more life into your space. Perhaps you want to rearrange them so you see more items that remind you of happy times.

7. As you're finishing, go through each room in the house and smudge it with palo santo or sage to move out the old energy and to make room for the new.

8. Finish by lighting a candle, closing your eyes, and sitting quietly and comfortably within your new space—the space you created on the outside and the one you're cultivating inside.

THE FIRST FULL MOON OF SPRING

ALTER YOUR ALTAR

Altars are a sacred symbol and have been a major part of ritual and worship for thousands of years. In the spirit of spring, we ask you to abandon all preconceived notions you have about what an altar "should be" to make room for what it is you need now. (For more on altar background and basics, refer to page 41.) Starting from square one, an altar is simply a reminder to you and your subconscious of your conscious intentions.

In the context of spring, the full moon's powerful energy provides the perfect opportunity to build a strong foundation for a year of intention with an altar. As plants emerge from the ground, fighting the elements and defying intense weather to bring new life to the environment, we take a cue from Mother Nature. Spring is a time to make yourself heard to the powers that be—even if it means going against your natural tendencies and stepping out of your comfort zone.

A PLACEMENT RITUAL FOR MANIFESTATION

One way to access your power is by refreshing your altar on the first full moon of spring.

These springtime altar essentials will form a medicine wheel—an homage to the cycles of life. Medicine wheels bring together the elements of water, fire, air, and earth, as reminders of cyclical renewal. Often seen as sacred in nature, they can imbue your altar with a meaningful connection to Mother Nature and the seasons.

WHAT YOU'LL NEED FROM THE OUTSIDE

* Twenty to seventy pieces of nature of varying sizes (Dried items will last longer than, say, leaves. Examples include pinecones, sea glass, leaves, shells, rocks, dried flowers, feathers, walnuts.)

- Feel free to use a combination of items.
- Make sure four of these items are larger than the rest.
* One object or small group of objects that symbolizes something you'd like to manifest
* Green cloth, paper, or tissue paper (any shade)

WHAT YOU'LL NEED FROM WITHIN

* Patience
* A clear spring vision
* The desire to get a little crafty

INSTRUCTIONS

1. Find a place for your medicine wheel on your altar or elsewhere in your home. If you're choosing a new place for your ritual altar or medicine wheel, try positioning it in the east part of your home, where the sun rises. If you broke a single day into seasons, dawn would be the spring.

2. Lay down your green cloth or paper. Green is a color that symbolizes fertility, nodding to the sea and the earth as sources of new life. It also stands for hope, regeneration, a new cycle, and luck.

3. Create a circle using your nature objects, with the four larger objects corresponding to the east, west, north, and south points like a compass. The circle symbolizes rebirth and renewal, and also follows the shape of the sun and the moon.

4. Using the remaining nature objects, make a line down the center of the circle. Then, make a line perpendicular to it so you've created four approximately equal sections. (If you don't have enough objects, feel free to skip this step and work with a circle.)

5. Place the object that symbolizes your dreams in the center. Set an intention, and mentally clarify or even write in your journal how

you'd like your dream to manifest. Indulge it, and imagine for a few minutes that it is true. It's said that the center of a medicine wheel is where the real world and the spirit world can commune with each other. Coupled with a full moon, this visualization method is an especially powerful practice.

Use your altar as a place to check in daily, weekly, or biweekly, reminding yourself of the intention you set. A medicine wheel is especially helpful if you're on the road—whether you want to make one in an inspiring natural landscape and leave it there, or travel with your stones and set up in your home away from home.

HOW TO KEEP IT GOING

Jenn Tardif, the founder and creator of 3rd Ritual, shares tips on how to ready your altar for spring. Since many rituals this season call for yoga and meditation, she will help you craft an altar to promote a quiet mind.

When I was working toward maintaining a daily at-home yoga practice, I experimented with leaving my mat and props permanently set up in the corner of my apartment. What was once a painful test of willpower (or lack thereof) quickly became an integral part of my daily routine. Like a toothbrush in the medicine cabinet, the mat and blocks were always ready and waiting to be used. Altars are similar. Humans are visual creatures, and having a permanent, sacred setup is like building a threshold for your spiritual practice to unfold, in whichever form that may take.

Altars are like snowflakes—each one is unique. It's important that they are as beautiful as they are significant, not just as an act of reverence for the divine but also for the practical reason that you'll be more inclined to sit in front of something inviting.

An Altar for Meditation

SUGGESTED OBJECTS

* A statue representative of your lineage (e.g., Shiva, Buddha)
* Your preferred meditation tool (e.g., mala beads or a sand timer)
* A candle for flame gazing
* A blend of vetiver, sandalwood, palo santo, and lavender essential oils (Note: You can lightly dab the blend behind your ears and on your wrists *or* simply smell it at the beginning of your sit to invite a deeper inhalation.)
* Your favorite stone (a crystal, a stone you collected on a hike, or a rock from a retreat) to help anchor you in the present moment
* An instrument such as a bell or chimes
* An object that represents your inner child
* An object that represents your future self
* A comfortable seat that encourages your hips to be higher than your knees, with soft padding between your feet and the floor

An Altar for Spring

SUGGESTED OBJECTS

* A vase with fresh, seasonal flowers (replenish as often as needed)
* Seeds to represent growth, expansion, and new beginnings
* Mist (such as jasmine or rose water) for purification
* A jade egg, representing new life
* Fabric with joyous colors and patterns for vibrancy
* Elements collected from nature (e.g., seashells, stones)
* An empty vessel to represent endless possibility

Note that spring is an ideal time to add music to your meditation or to try chanting or humming while you sit. (For more on a humming ritual, see page 206.)

NATIONAL TEA DAY

(APRIL 21)

TEATIME

Let's face it: Sometimes tea gets a bad rap! Coffee has long been portrayed as the sexier, more mysterious and desirable of the two, but today's British holiday aims to celebrate tea drinking. And it's fitting—the British are known for teatime, many thanks to Catherine of Braganza, who hailed from Portugal and married King Charles II in 1662, bringing tea to the country. The tradition of tea drinking didn't catch on until the 1800s, though, when tea became affordable to the masses.

Teatime, or Elevenses, happens, as you might guess, at 11:00 in the morning and is meant to be a midmorning break with dry pastries such as biscuits and scones. It is strongly associated with J. R. R. Tolkien's work because hobbits loved any excuse to eat, but Elevenses existed long before that. Afternoon tea, on the other hand, is served between 3:00 and 4:00 in the afternoon, and was originally a ritual enjoyed exclusively by England's upper class. Because royalty often took afternoon tea in cushy armchairs and couches, it was actually called low tea. High tea originated with the working class, because they were situated at proper dinner tables—literally higher off the ground than the upper class's low, loungy teatime. Laborers didn't have the luxury of taking a midday break, so they had tea with dinner soon after the workday was over.

The Brits made tea a cultural norm, but the tea ceremony is rich with ancient history and ritual that predates them. It's nearly impossible to trace the origin of tea, but we know it was used medicinally in Shanghai, China, in about 2700 BC. Fast-forward to the present day, and matcha tea—one of the world's new favorites—was popularized by Japan's ancient tea ceremonies that involved a special, ritualized preparation and presentation of matcha for entertainment and gathering, both formal and casual.

A TASSOLOGY RITUAL FOR INSIGHT

Drinking tea has always been a ceremonial, ritualized, and connective experience—all qualities that lend themselves well to divination. Here's an informal primer on how to read your own tea leaves, a practice known as tassology. While predictive exercises like this can be daunting, we advise taking them with a grain of salt. You're the maker of your destiny, not your teacup, but perhaps your cup can point you in the right direction. Like beauty, your future is in the eye of the beholder.

WHAT YOU'LL NEED FROM THE OUTSIDE

* A cup of loose-leaf tea
* A journal, or use the blank pages found in the beginning of this season

WHAT YOU'LL NEED FROM WITHIN

* A steady gaze into the future
* The willingness to tap into your intuition

INSTRUCTIONS

1. Brew a cup of tea using your favorite loose tea leaves or one of the recipes from Dages Juvelier Keates on page 118, but instead of using a strainer, keep it loose.
2. Make a little moment out of drinking your tea. Get comfy and settled. You can do this while reading a book, journaling, or chatting with a friend. Do anything you wish, as long as you're staying present.

3. When you've got just a few sips left, swirl the water around a few times and drink the remaining tea.

4. Swirl a few more times and let your leaves settle.

5. Start to take note of the shapes you see and how they map to the cup, referring to the abbreviated symbols in the "Leaves of Change" box.

6. In your own interpretation, write a journal entry describing what you see. Make sure to write down the date so you can come back to the entry later to see how true it was.

7. Once you try this exercise on yourself, see if a friend is willing to let you read her leaves!

LEAVES OF CHANGE

Here is a primer on how to decode the symbols you may find in your cup, adapted from the original text, *Reading Tea Leaves* by "A Highland Seer."

* What shapes and symbols do you see in the bottom of your cup? These signify the future.

* What shapes and symbols do you see near the rim of the cup? These indicate something in the near future.

* Notice the orientation of shapes. Are they moving toward or away from something?

* If you see any letters, they usually stand for someone's name and should be read in the context of other signals.

* Like letters, if you see numbers, look to them to define or add context to surrounding shapes.

* Look at the overall pattern of the leaves. Are they grouped, defined, and splotchy? This cup probably has a lot to say. Are they disparate, making almost no shape at all? This cup means the person drinking it is overextended. Do they create wavy lines? Those are indicative of the journey in the context of other symbols.

And here is a (very) abbreviated list of common tassology symbols:

Angel: good news, particularly in love

Flying bird: an important message is coming your way

Bat: a project or journey won't reap rewards

Circles: money or gifts

Crescent moon: incoming prosperity

Flowers: success, a happy relationship, or good fortune

House: a successful project

Triangles: emphasize the symbols around them, especially with good luck

Lion: powerful friends will help you succeed

Snake: a bad omen

Unicorn: a scandal

Zebra: travel to distant lands

HOW TO KEEP IT GOING

Yoga teacher, herbal medicine maker, meditation guide, and artist Dages Juvelier Keates has shared three tea recipes to help transition the body through the spring season, each brewed with information from Dages's teacher and mentor, Robin Rose Bennett.

There are a few important things to keep in mind when making herbal tonics. Placing your glass jar on a wooden cutting board prevents the jar from cracking with the temperature change. When the herbs are done steeping, remember that it's the inside of the plant that holds the green gold! If you'd prefer not to get your hands dirty, line your strainer with cheesecloth, gather the edges, and squeeze your medicinal brew this way. And always compost your plant material when you're done.

Early Spring: Green Gold Infusion

Nettles pack a real punch. Brush them and it can feel like being stung by a bee, but drinking them can make you feel like royalty! Invigorating, deeply nourishing, and loaded with protein, calcium, and energy-enhancing vitamins and minerals, nettles will help you shed winter doldrums by lifting spirits, enhancing sleep, and potentiating your body's systems. If you're wildcrafting, these magnificent plants should be harvested before they blossom. Use gloves to avoid their fiery kiss (which can be rash-inducing).

INGREDIENTS

* Dried wildcrafted nettles (get these at your local herb shop or at Mountain Rose Herbs online store)
* A one-quart glass jar
* Chopstick or wooden spoon
* Sieve
* Cheesecloth *(optional)*
* Ice, lemon, and miso and/or umeboshi paste *(optional)*

DIRECTIONS

1. Fill a one-quart jar ¼ full of dried nettles.
2. Pour boiling water over the dried plant material. Stir with a chopstick or wooden spoon, and top off with more water. Cap tightly.
3. Allow to steep for eight hours or overnight.
4. Put the drink through a strainer, wringing out the herb matter using your hands or a cheesecloth.
5. Your now-room-temperature potion can be enjoyed as is, poured over ice to cool things off further (try adding a bit of lemon!), reheated for a warming tea, or made into a salty broth with the addition of miso and/or umeboshi paste.

A note on storage: Due to its protein-packed goodness, a nettle infusion will last only two days in the fridge, tightly capped. Extend its life by freezing your infusion in an ice cube tray. Pop one into a warm soup or dilute it with hot water for a nourishing medicinal drink.

Mid-Spring: Roots to Rise Infusion

This infusion is potent, since four herbs are working together to detoxify the system. Burdock is a blood cleanser and strengthens the liver and kidneys. Dandelion root and violet bring nourishment and cool the liver, and red clover is high in protein and helps with digestion.

INGREDIENTS

* ½ ounce burdock
* ½ ounce dandelion
* ½ ounce red clover
* ½ ounce violet
* A one-quart glass jar
* Chopstick or wooden spoon
* Sieve
* Honey *(optional)*
* Cheesecloth *(optional)*

DIRECTIONS

1. Fill a one-quart jar ¼ full of dried herb mixture.
2. Pour boiling water over the dried plant material.
3. Stir with a chopstick or wooden spoon, and top off with more water. Cap tightly.
4. Allow to steep for eight hours or overnight.
5. Put the drink through a strainer, wringing out the herb matter using your hands or a cheesecloth.
6. Compost your plant material, and enjoy the brew!

LATE SPRING: FALL VIOLET BLOSSOM HONEY

Vibrant violet is a delightful harbinger of spring, her white, blue, purple, and yellow flowers announcing warmer weather and the beauty of blossoming. Gentle, cooling, and potent, violet stimulates lymph, supports immunity, and moves out dry, stagnant residual gunk from our winter ways. Slippery, soothing, and mucilaginous, this ally works on our digestive, respiratory, urinary, and nervous systems.

INGREDIENTS

* Clean, sterile, dry jar with a tight-fitting lid
* Fresh violet blossoms from your local farmers market (Do not wash them, as water can cause your honey to spoil.)
* Local high-quality honey
* Chopstick

DIRECTIONS

1. Fill the clean jar with your fresh, dry violets.
2. Cover with honey.
3. Use a chopstick to poke the herb material down. See all those bubbles? Keep poking and top off your potion with more honey.
4. Lid the jar and turn it upside down a few times. Check to see if you need to top it off again.
5. Look in on your potion over the next few days to see if you need to add more honey as the blossoms settle.
6. If you can, wait four to six weeks for optimum taste. If not, enjoy it sooner!

ℰARTH DAY

☾ (APRIL 22)

LOVE YOUR MOTHER

Mother Earth, first named by the Greeks for her fertility and ability to support life, is an expansive embodiment of the feminine spirit. She is moody and cyclical while incredibly strong and resolute. Men and women gawk at her beauty, photographing her from all angles and in all lights. Some have fought wars for her; others have dedicated their lives to chasing her up and down. She has peaks and valleys, coastlines and deserts, and we have found home in them all. And yet, as we continue to take, Mother Earth is losing the ability to give.

We've lost sight of the reciprocity of it all, forgetting that we must show Earth the love she has so selflessly shown us. Reminders of our greed now exist at every turn: extreme storms, wildfires, and dead zones all fueled by climate change. We have clogged her air, polluted her water, and destroyed her grandeur in an indomitable quest for something we'll never even find—happiness by way of the material. The great irony is that true joy comes from working with the earth, not against her. It comes from enjoying the gifts she has to offer instead of destroying them to make gifts of our own.

Needless to say, forging meaningful connections with the earth is more important today than ever before. For inspiration on how to do so, we can look toward those who have always lived in beautiful communion with our planet.

Many indigenous cultures are stewards of the earth, and Native Americans are a particularly poignant example. They are a people who have always celebrated the spirit in all creatures and revere nature as a sacred place that feeds us. They fought to protect land from newcomers, and their warnings have come to invigorate and inspire the environmental movement today.

"Only when the last tree has died, and the last river has been poisoned, and the last fish has been caught, will we realize that we cannot eat money," reads one Native proverb.

A CRYSTAL RITUAL FOR GROUNDING

The first Earth Day, in 1970, brought twenty million Americans to the streets to protest environmental pollution. Now nearly two hundred countries have joined the rallying cry and the day has turned into a global occasion to protect nature's magnificence. While we believe that every day should be Earth Day, let's use the holiday to come back to our devotion to the planet. This quick ritual will serve as a reminder of all that the earth has given you and all that you can give back to her.

WHAT YOU'LL NEED FROM THE OUTSIDE

* A crystal of your choice, one that you don't mind parting with

WHAT YOU'LL NEED FROM WITHIN

* Memories of your fondest days spent admiring Mother Nature

INSTRUCTIONS

1. Today, head out somewhere wild, crystal in hand. Take off your shoes and feel the ground beneath your feet. Tactile connection with the earth has been shown in some studies to help our bodies function optimally—and we believe it. Nature, after all, is where we are always home.
2. Hold your crystal in both of your hands and take some deep breaths. For the next few moments, visualize some of your favorite memories from being outside, beginning with childhood—almost as if you're playing back a movie of your life. Feeling the strong hold of the earth and squeezing your crystal all the while, say, "The earth supports me,

and I support the earth," at the end of each memory. Like Native American tribes who shape their rituals around gratitude for the world around them, give thanks for all that it has given you. Continue the exercise until you arrive at the present day.

3. Spend one last minute visualizing all those earthly memories flooding up from the ground, through your body, and into the crystal in your hand. Once you have "programmed" your crystal, dig up a patch of land and leave it as an offering to the earth from which it came.

4. Then, decide on a practical way to thank Mother Nature for her offerings. Pick up any trash you see on your walk home, or donate to an environmental organization once you get back to your computer. Gratitude for nature is no longer enough. It needs to be followed by action, always.

HOW TO KEEP IT GOING

Here are a few ideas on how you can make a long-term ritual of protecting the earth.

* USE YOUR MONEY MINDFULLY. Re-create the piggy banks of childhood by dropping any loose change or bills you have at the end of the week into a jar or bowl. Instead of spending this money on the material, you'll be paying it back to the land. Once your vessel is full, make a donation to one of the amazing organizations fighting for the future of our planet. Our top picks are the Natural Resources Defense Council, the Nature Conservancy, and Sierra Club.

* WRITE FOR CHANGE. Channel some of those memories you uncovered in your Earth Day ritual into a letter to your local government representative, explaining why environmental protection means so much to you. At least in the United States, these personal anecdotes make politicians far more likely to actually read your note instead of just piling it in with all the rest. Every time you feel called—whether you're triggered by the beauty of the natural world or an attack against it—write another letter. It's one of the quickest, easiest ways to claim your voice.

* **SNAP A SHOT**. Your camera (or iPhone, if used correctly) can be the ultimate reminder to stay present. Every day for at least month, take a photograph outside. It doesn't need to capture a sweeping vista or vibrant rainbow. Any piece of nature that made you stop in your tracks—a branch, the first budding of flowers, a cloud formation—will do just fine. The important piece is remembering to slow down and let your surroundings inspire you every day.

MAY DAY

☾ (MAY 1)

SUPER NATURAL

May Day has always been a celebration of spring. In the late 1800s and early 1900s, people would gather flowers, sweets, and other small niceties into a handmade paper basket for someone they admired. Come the first of May, they'd sneak up the steps, hang the basket on his or her doorknob, ring the doorbell, and run away. It was a chance for young ones to express love and, if they were lucky, to feel it reciprocated.

Another tradition of May Day is the beautiful maypole. A tall, wooden pole with ribbons hanging from the top was used in ceremonies by Germanic Europeans in medieval times. Anyone participating in the maypole ceremony (often called a maypole dance) would grab a ribbon and walk around the pole, eventually creating a spiral decoration on the pole. These modern interpretations of May Day were said to have been born from Beltane, a Germanic holiday, or Walpurgis Night, a pagan celebration, before they lost their religious connotations.

More recently, May Day has also become associated with socialism and communism, as it's been deemed International Workers' Day, but that's a story for another day and time.

A BOTANICAL ARRANGEMENT RITUAL FOR ENERGY

To nod to May Day traditions of times past, let's take today to pick and arrange foraged flowers—even if all you find are a few dead tree branches. Every time you see your arrangement, you'll be reminded of the beauty in nature's bounty.

WHAT YOU NEED FROM THE OUTSIDE

* Comfortable walking shoes
* Scissors
* A vessel for flowers

WHAT YOU NEED FROM WITHIN

* An eye for beauty in the mundane

INSTRUCTIONS

1. Identify a place where you'll run into a few different species of plant flora. This may be your backyard or a nearby park, but make sure you have permission to pick from it.
2. Steer clear of poison ivy and sumac! Familiarize yourself with what they look like before you go. You know the rule: Leaves of three, let them be.
3. Pack a canvas or cloth bag, a pair of gloves, and some scissors.
4. Without any preconceived notions of what you want your arrangement to look like, head out on a walk to see what you find.
5. Weather permitting, walk for a while to give yourself a chance to look closely at the beauty of what you'd normally pass right by. Begin to forage any plants that catch your eye.
6. Stop and smell the roses—literally. Spend a few minutes in each little pocket of nature and pay attention to your senses: How does it smell,

sound, feel, and look? Take photos if you fancy, to inspire your arrangement.

7. Once you've foraged enough, head back home and take out your vase or vessel, filling it halfway with water. Begin clipping stems, trimming branches, and arranging. Instead of trying to force beauty, let your objects shine for what they are.

LET YOUR FREAK FLAG FLY

Instead of chasing the "perfect" flora bouquet, take a cue from ikebana, the Japanese art of flower arranging that lets asymmetry and minimalism shine through. It's a joyful celebration of the raw elements of nature, not an attempt to freeze them into a neat little package. Here are some ideas to keep in mind as you're fashioning your creation.

✳ Consider how your arrangement takes up space, both vertically and horizontally. Do you want to grow up or out?

✳ If you don't find many flowers, let other items steal the show. Try mixing your blooms with branches and withered leaves.

✳ If you want to take it a step further, cut a block of foam small enough to fit in your vessel. Poke stems in it, orienting them at different angles into a kind of abstract art instillation.

✳ In ikebana, the spiritual, mindful element of flower arranging is revered. Challenge yourself to live in the moment and find a bit of grandeur in everything as you add to your display.

HOW TO KEEP IT GOING

Here, herbalist and natural beauty expert Jessa Blades shares how to harness the power of flower essences in spring. (For a refresher on these essences, head over to page 82.)

As the earth wakes up in the spring, all we have to look to is the plants for inspiration. Flower essences are a reliable way to feel grounded and connected to the earth after the cozy quiet of winter. Flowers are so versatile. You can incorporate them into food or drink, use dried ones in teas or honeys, or include them in your self-care rituals.

Ingesting or making flower essences from spring plants is a beautiful way to interact with a subtle form of energy medicine that can have deeply powerful and transformative effects. Here are some of the best flower essences for spring, cherry blossom and crocus.

1. **CHERRY BLOSSOM ESSENCE**: Cherry blossom is a sweet essence that promotes joy in life, helping you open your heart toward innocence and wonder. It is said to help release doubt, negativity, and that which does not serve, so you can move toward hitting the refresh button, so to speak. They allow you to see the vast potential in all the beauty that surrounds you, making them a great essence to use in your springtime manifestation rituals.

2. **CROCUS ESSENCE**: Crocus comes around at first thaw and sometimes even pops up through snow. This essence is great to move energy that is hard or stuck. Use crocus to support you in an area of your life that could use renewal or a do-over. Let it help you push through change and show you how to open up to abundance.

Although flowers are typically fragrant when harvested, their essences have no scent and barely any taste, and are generally safe for children and pets (aside from known allergies). I'd recommend an average dose of one to four drops up to four times per day, taken directly on your tongue or in your water. Another option is to massage the essence on your wrists or over your heart.

World Laughter Day

G (FIRST SUNDAY OF MAY)

LET IT GO

World Laughter Day, which falls on the first Sunday of May, promotes the idea of laughing for its own sake—simply because it feels good. It pays homage to a movement started in 1998 by Dr. Madan Kataria, the "laughing guru," who wanted to raise awareness of laughter's health benefits. He's also the brains and the belly laugh behind laughter yoga (exactly what it sounds like), which has benefited hundreds of thousands of people around the world. In addition to running an ashram founded on laughter yoga, he trains other teachers so they can start "laughter clubs"—gatherings where people get together to laugh, goof off, and have a good time.

And while limited evidence is available, therapeutic laughter shows promise. Laughter, like smiling, is one of the most universally understood expressions of emotion. It's been shown to strengthen human connections; reduce anxiety, depression, and stress in breast cancer patients; and lower blood sugar and blood pressure. While doctors haven't figured out exactly why, there are a few theories: It boosts mood-improving neurotransmitters; it increases nitric oxide in artery walls, which helps with blood pressure; or it could be because it engages the diaphragm and the muscles around it, which may help regulate stress hormones.

So go ahead, laugh it off.

A DIAPHRAGMATIC BREATHING RITUAL FOR RELEASE

In addition to regularly laughing, engaging your diaphragm through breathwork can help you release stagnation in the body. You can use the following breathwork exercises to multiply the potency of other springtime rituals, and it's especially helpful when you're feeling blocked or stuck. It'll also help you recognize whether you have what's known as a reverse breathing pattern, which can cause anxiety, and can guide you on how to correct it.

WHAT YOU'LL NEED FROM THE OUTSIDE

* A yoga mat, rug, or blanket that makes lying on the floor comfortable

WHAT YOU'LL NEED FROM WITHIN

* Laser focus and concentration. No easy ask, but you'll get the hang of it.

INSTRUCTIONS

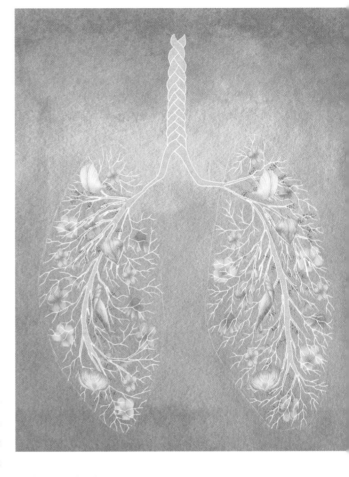

1. Lying down on your yoga mat, rug, or blanket, breathe normally. You can extend your legs long (the preferred position, as it stretches your psoas slightly) or keep them bent here, whichever is more comfortable for your back.
2. Notice as you breathe in whether your chest or your belly rises. If your chest rises as you breathe in, you have a reverse breathing pattern. This keeps the breath in the chest and doesn't properly engage the diaphragm. Over time, this can lead to a buildup of anxiety and stress.
3. Breathe in through your nose and out through your mouth. Now, as you breathe in, inflate your belly like a balloon. It may feel strange if you're not used to it. Go slowly and inhale to an easy count of three; then exhale to the same count.

4. After a few rounds of belly breathing, start to engage more of your lungs. After inflating your belly, slowly move up to your rib cage and go wide with breath, expanding. After breathing wide in your torso, bring the breath high, right up to your collarbones. As you exhale, let all the breath fall out of you.

5. Keep going like this, inhaling so a beat goes low into the belly, another beat expands your rib cage wide, and another inflates your lungs high. Allow the exhale to tumble out of you. Do this three to five times.

6. If you start to feel a little tingly, it's normal. You're flooding your system with oxygen. Of course, if you feel uncomfortable, feel free to relax into your normal breath.

7. Now return to your normal breath for a minute or so and feel how, just by breathing differently, you were able to shift your own energy.

8. As you feel ready, slowly turn over to your right side. Take your time as you push up to sit. As usual, write down any thoughts or feelings, or describe your experience in your journal if you feel called.

HOW TO KEEP IT GOING

Ramesh Tarun Narine, a craniosacral therapist, registered massage therapist, meditation guide, and yoga teacher, has honed his healing practice to the art of reading and tuning the nervous system. Here, he shares a home practice you can do to improve vagal nerve tone. Practicing active but restorative breathwork and movements allows you to participate in your body's regulation of the stress response.

These simple techniques inform you (and your body) of where your breath is moving. They can help you cultivate a more mindful engagement of the breath—one that is smooth, harmonious, and rhythmic. If you reach a need to gasp for breath with any of them, you've gone too far.

MAKRASANA

This is also known as crocodile pose. Expect to stay here for a minimum of five minutes.

1. Lying on your stomach with your legs wider than your hips, point your toes outward.
2. Fold your arms in front of your body so that your chest isn't touching the ground and place your hands on your biceps.
3. Rest your forehead comfortably on the backs of your stacked arms.
4. Bring your attention to your abdomen.
5. Notice your belly breath, your diaphragmatic breath.
6. Your inhale presses your abdomen into the floor. Observe your lower rib cage expanding.
7. Look for a fluid movement in your diaphragm, free of jerks.
8. As you exhale, feel your abdominal muscles relax. This movement is free of effort.
9. Notice changes in the state of your relaxation.
10. To come out of the pose, inhale and bring your legs together, turning your right cheek to the floor as your arms reach overhead. Take a few breaths. Bring your arms beside your body as you turn your left cheek to the floor. Breathe. Roll onto your back, spending a few breaths in savasana or another final resting pose.

1:1 AND 1:2 BREATHING

This is a great exercise to work on over time so you can play around with different lengths and ratios.

1. Begin with a simple 1:1 ratio. Count a four-beat inhale and a four-beat exhale, expanding through your belly, rib cage, and collarbone like you did in the Makrasana ritual.
2. Start to expand this number, or stay with four if you're new to the practice. If you're expanding, begin with a small increase that you can maintain for five minutes. Once this is comfortable, expand the count to five, to six, to seven. . . . This may happen over time and with practice, not all in one session.
3. When you're confident doing this, play with a 1:2 breath ratio. A 1:2 ratio is a four-count inhale and an eight-count exhale. Pursing your

lips creates a little resistance, supporting the lengthened exhale. Doing this for two to three minutes stimulates the diaphragm. If you're pregnant, stick with 1:1 breathing.

LEGS UP THE WALL

Sixty percent of your body's blood supply is stored in your legs, so anytime you can use gravity to assist your heart in that effort, it's rejuvenating. This passive pose is meant to be full of ease once you get into it.

1. With a few folded blankets against a wall, begin on your right side in the fetal position, keeping pressure off your heart, with your tail toward the wall and your head away from it. Place your sitz bones, the bony part of your butt, against the wall, just to the side of the blankets, and roll onto your back, bringing your tail to an elevated position on the props.
2. Straighten your legs up the wall and place one hand on your chest and one hand on your abdomen. Watching your belly rise and fall as your chest remains still, practice maintaining your awareness in your abdomen and breathing diaphragmatically.
3. To come out of the pose gently, reverse the steps.

Practicing these simple skills on their own or in any sequence will support you as you develop awareness of your breath and vagal tone. Check in with a medical professional, particularly if you have high or low blood pressure, before regularly including these in your routine.

MOTHER'S DAY

(SECOND SUNDAY OF MAY)

WOMB TO GROW

The tale of Mother's Day started in in the nineteenth century, before the Civil War. A woman by the name of Ann Reeves Jarvis hailing from West Virginia hosted mothers' clubs to teach local moms how best to care for their kids. Once the war began, she encouraged mothers from both Confederate and Union families to commingle, promoting peace among former soldiers, their children, and one another. She continued promoting peace and healthy relationships among mothers and children, and it was her dying wish that Mother's Day become an official commemoration for mothers.

While it's unclear whether Ann imagined a day to honor your own mother or a day for all mothers, her daughter, Anna, made it her life's mission to make the day official. And she did. It took several years, hundreds of letters to government representatives, and campaigning, but President Woodrow Wilson eventually signed a bill passing it as a federal holiday in 1914. By that time, several states were already celebrating it.

Unfortunately, what should have been a victory for Anna ended up turning on her. She'd envisioned Mother's Day as a special day where children were meant to honor mothers with praise and gratitude, but holiday card companies and florists soon started profiting from her life's work. It ultimately affected her health as well as her emotional and physical well-being and drained her until she passed in 1948. It's quite the sad story, but reviving the original idea of Mother's Day—appreciating the woman and women and womyn who mothered you, without worrying about material gifts—would have made Anna proud.

DAYBREAK WOMB RITUAL FOR CREATIVITY

This Mother's Day ritual involves celebrating the divine mother in all of us, no matter your gender. Tapping into the quiet power of dawn and the birth of a new day, we'll tune in to our bodies to reveal our truths and how we so often get in our own way. Everyone is a mother to their own projects, ideas, and dreams. As we move into the vibrant summer season, let's identify what these are for you and how you can bring them into being.

WHAT YOU'LL NEED FROM THE OUTSIDE

* Warm clothing if it's chilly where you are
* Your alarm clock
* A morning beverage
* A pen
* Your journal

WHAT YOU'LL NEED FROM WITHIN

* Sensitivity
* A sense of nurturing

INSTRUCTIONS

1. Set your alarm clock to go off a half hour before the sunrise—it should already be getting close to daybreak when you wake. You can stay at home or go somewhere scenic; just be wary of your surroundings.
2. Settle into your space, and admire the colors that paint each and every morning. Remind yourself that there are seasons even within days, and spring is the dawn.
3. Notice the colors of the sky today, and perhaps remember the last time you watched the sun rise. How is your life different now? How do you wish it were different?

4. Turn your attention to your womb space. This is in your belly, under your diaphragm and above your sex organs. When we're creating authentically, we do it from this space.

5. Listen. What is digging at the pit of your belly? Are there suppressed desires still brewing? Is there a really good feeling about a person, place, or thing? Breathe and notice.

6. Now think of the miracle that is you. Think of your mother, and your mother's mother, and your mother's mother's mother, and so on. Acknowledge the creation—not only conception, pregnancy, and birthing but the work—that has all left its imprint on you.

7. You are a part of this miracle. But you're also a mother to your own ideas, projects, and creativity. Explore what is keeping you from creating what you want, what is keeping you from creating at all, and what drives you to create.

8. As the sun continues to rise, write down anything that comes up. Tap into the energy of your ancestors to support your creation. Writing is a way to express the power, desires, and energy of the divine mother within you. What's left on the page doesn't need to make sense for the exercise to be effective.

It's normal to cry, release, or feel things that aren't necessarily positive when you're in a womb space exploring blocks. You may not even fully understand your emotions, and that's okay! Just let them flow, write them down, and be sure to experience them. By holding space for this energy, we allow it to move through us, lifting our blocks. Ultimately these experiences give us vital information and insight on how to move forward with projects, relationships, and the journey.

HOW TO KEEP IT GOING

Natalia Hailes and Ashley Spivak, doulas, reproductive health educators, and founders of Brilliant Bodies and CYCLES + SEX, have offered a more physical way to sync with your womb space—the fertility awareness method.

This method taps into the magic of the feminine body and explores how it changes through its own cycles.

It can be inspiring and empowering to reinvent your relationship with your body by learning the rhythms of your own menstrual cycle. There's so much power that can come from understanding how your body works, how your emotional state can correspond to the changes in your cycle (why at some times you may feel the need to be very social and at others, stay home hiding under the covers), and how to use all these signs to your advantage as a way to reconnect with your body.

Start with a cycle journal, using tenets of the Fertility Awareness Method. Here's how you can turn it into a daily self-discovery ritual:

Start by tracking the following categories: temperature, cervical fluid, skin (e.g., breakouts, clarity, sensitivity), stomach (e.g., state of digestion), cervix, blood, emotional state, and other.

1. When you wake up each morning, resist the urge to get out of bed immediately or look at your phone. Instead, take your temperature (orally) and write it down.

2. When you're ready for your first morning pee, wash your hands and check the quality of your cervical fluid by inserting your fingers inside and taking a look at what comes out. Is it sticky, creamy, pasty, milky, lotiony, or even stretchy when tacked between your finger pads? Write it down. If you are bleeding, note the quality and color of the blood. Is it brown, light pink, bright red? Is it watery, syrupy, or clumpy?

3. Before you get out of the shower, squat down and find your cervix. Does it feel more open or closed? Soft or hard? Is it closer or harder to reach? Take note.

4. Find at least two other times throughout the day you can check in with your physical and emotional state and, if you can, even your cervical fluid or blood, if you're ovulating. Take note if you feel particularly stressed or hungry, have pain in a certain area, or feel sad, inspired, social, bloated, crampy, broken out, etc.

Write everything down. Doing this for a few months can help give you clues into what's ailing you, whether it's skin woes, headaches, mental meltdowns, digestive issues, or fatigue. As you take notice of these daily changes, you'll get a much better understanding of how your cycle works and of the patterns that may arise. Bring this information to your doctor if you're investigating your health. If you want to practice the Fertility Awareness Method to conceive or avoid pregnancy, though, we highly recommend working with a licensed practitioner to help you get a better sense of how it works and what each sign means for your individual body.

Summer

I come into the peace of wild things
who do not tax their lives with forethought of grief. . . .
I rest in the grace of the world, and am free.
—WENDELL BERRY

SUMMER COMES AT JUST THE RIGHT TIME. Following months of hibernation and regeneration, this season's return reminds us to admire everything we've been so busy planting. Summer is the fiery crescendo of the year's cycle, a period defined by energy and excess. School is out, vacations abound, and schedules loosen as we rush to get outside to take in the warmth we thought we'd lost. We shed more solitary existences for social ones as chatter and laughter become the background track to months lived in vibrant color. While the start of seasons past felt like wading into a cloudy unknown, this is a whole lot more like dancing into the light.

Summer: A History

As they did with the winter solstice, our ancestors rang in the summer solstice with spectacle. Native American tribes welcomed it with a sacred sun dance passed along through generations. Over in Scandinavia, midsummer was an occasion to feast on the new bounty, embrace nature with floral crowns and bouquets, and sometimes take another whirl or two around spring's maypole. Across the rest of Europe and America, bonfires lit up the dusk as people set out to gather the medicinal herbs that were believed to be at their most potent this time of year. Legend has it that magical spirits also arrived with the coming of summer, as evidenced by the mischievous fairies in Shakespeare's *A Midsummer Night's Dream.*

Once the initial merriment and magic wore off, summer became a time of work as well as play. In agrarian societies, it meant long days sweating in the field collecting crops. Poetically enough, the natural world around us needs to push a little harder during the season too. In peak summer months, honeybees fly far and wide to collect pollen and nectar from the flowers that are also working to bloom with the sunshine. But with this work came reprieve. Medieval summer hunts were followed by feasts in the forests, the prelude to what we now call picnics, and the first modern Olympic Games in nineteenth-century Athens paired athletic feats with celebrations of tribe and nation. It's no wonder the word "summer" has been traced to the root "sem," meaning together as one.

THE SEASON'S SIGNIFICANCE

The Chinese five-element system splits summer into two parts. Early summer takes on the fire element, with its passion, intensity, and friction. While captivating, this fire can spiral out of control if we're not careful—just as burning the candle at both ends becomes a very real possibility in the jampacked season. Late summer, on the other hand, is associated with the earth element of settling, grounding, and reconnecting with our roots in preparation for fall. It's a moment to come back down to reality following a period spent looking outward and upward.

Summer is the yang to winter's yin, full of masculine, relentless energy. Eastern medicine warns that we need to hold on to a bit of yin's slowness and ease to balance out our summers, or we'll end up dehydrated, exhausted, and generally overextended. Moral of the story: Celebrate the season's energizing fire, but rein it in when necessary.

If it were a moon phase, summer would be a full moon, without a doubt. It's a period when everything is amplified and emotions run wild. We can perceive it as either overwhelming and frenetic, or an empowering time of self-reflection. Just as the full moon is an opportunity to reassess our goals according to the lunar calendar, summer is a time to do so under the seasonal one. As your emotions rise more clearly to the surface this season, it's up to you to listen to them and identify whatever needs to go in your life—then release it.

MODERN SUMMER RITUAL

Summertime holidays vary widely around the world, but many of them share the same undertones of community and pride. The United States and Canada celebrate their independence with fireworks and parades in summer, while in East Asia people gather to race in the Duanwu (Dragon Boat) Festival as a show of national unity. The French celebrate their country with Bastille Day in July while celebrations of independence take the streets of Burundi, Somalia, and Rwanda that same month.

In America, lighthearted holidays such as Friendship Day, Book Lovers Day, and Kissing Day have also been added to our summertime calendars over the years. It's fitting that a season defined by energy, togetherness, and play now holds celebrations that follow suit.

SUMMER IS A TIME TO . . .

* Socialize and pinpoint the people and experiences that make you feel happy and free.

* Live less in your to-do list and more in your bucket list.

* Take the long way home.

* Check in on your goals and reassess anything that needs to shift.

* Make room for childhood play and movement, hiding and seeking.

No matter where you live in the world, summer represents the crest of the year's cycle—the culmination of all that we built in winter and spring. Therefore, this season's rituals should help us revel in all that we've created while taking note of what's working about it and what isn't. May these rituals inspire you to sing along to the chorus of the year's song while also thinking about how its notes could ring a little sweeter.

THE SUMMER SOLSTICE

STEP INTO THE SUN

During the summer solstice in the United States, the sun shines everywhere from thirteen and a half hours in Miami to nearly sixteen hours as you move up to Seattle. Farther north of the equator, Stockholm is flooded with eighteen and a half hours of light, and the day lasts an incredible twenty-one hours in Reykjavik, with the sun rising just before 3:00 a.m. and setting a few moments after midnight.

Those before us fervently celebrated the gods and goddesses who brought this nearly limitless sunshine, and odes to them still exist today. Apollo, the Greek god of the sun, is a common figure in folklore, shining light alongside his twin sister, Artemis, the goddess of the moon. Considered a symbol of immense beauty, Apollo was celebrated across much of the ancient world, and he was the muse for one of the very first Roman temples. In Japanese culture, Amaterasu is the goddess of the sun as well as the greater universe. Legend has it that at one point, she became angry and locked herself in a cave, which engulfed the world in darkness and made way for evil spirits. The Ise Grand Shrine, a revered shrine in the Shinto religion, is dedicated to the sun goddess and the way we depend on her to show us the path forward.

A FREE—FORM DRAWING RITUAL FOR MAGNIFICENCE

Let's head outside to take in the seemingly never-ending sunshine on the day of this year's solstice (or shortly afterward, weather permitting). Considering this season's theme of social activity balanced with a mindful appreciation of our surroundings, it makes sense to kick things off with one big ode to nature—the dandelions taking to the field, the fireflies taking to the night, and the greenery that's getting more and more lush with each passing day.

WHAT YOU'LL NEED FROM THE OUTSIDE

* A journal, or just use the blank pages found in the beginning of this season
* A pen
* A blanket, cushion, or something to sit on
* Colored pencils/art materials *(optional)*

WHAT YOU'LL NEED FROM WITHIN

* An excitement to get outside
* A sharpness of mind to pay more attention to the things you usually just brush past
* Your sense of creativity

INSTRUCTIONS

1. Grab your paper and pen and find an area outside where you can sit comfortably for a while. It can be a place that consistently strikes you with its beauty, but we think this exercise is more powerful when it's someplace you pass every day but never really stop to admire.

2. Sit up straight and start easing into your breath. Closing your eyes if you wish, breathe in for four counts, hold for two (if you're pregnant, skip the hold), and exhale for four. With each inhale, see if you can notice something new about your space—the rustle of leaves, the sound of bikes passing by, the way the wind hits your face, or the smells of the summer air. Repeat for a few moments, until your mind begins to anchor and you start to feel more present than when you first sat down.

3. Open your eyes if they were shut, grab your pen, and, beginning with the first thing that catches your gaze, draw the scene around you *without looking down at the paper.* Continue to keep your gaze upward, with the intention of noticing even the tiniest details. Let your

mind guide the pen. If you feel an urge to look down at first, ignore it and keep going. Allow yourself the freedom to create without concern for beauty or aesthetic. There's something really liberating about just doing and expressing.

4. Once you feel as though your scene is complete, look down at the page and write out a simple "Thank you" where you see a blank space, or on the back. It's a thank-you to yourself for doing something that might make you a bit uneasy, a thank-you to the world around you for providing endless inspiration, and a thank-you to the new season for all that it has yet to bring.

No matter what the end product looks like, let it remind you to slow down this summer and soak in the grace and details that are easy to miss.

HOW TO KEEP IT GOING

Artist and owner of Flora Bowley Designs, Flora Bowley is a firm believer that creative expression can promote healing and holistic well-being. Here, she guides us through a few of her favorite outdoor drawing exercises, which you can practice all year long to slow down and appreciate the wild world around you.

1. **DRAW THE SHADOWS**. Drawing shadows is a simple, easy way to capture unique shapes and images with a little help from the sun. Head outside and start to see where the light and shadows meet. Notice what shadow shapes feel interesting to you, and place your sketchbook in the path of these shadows so they fall on your page. Trace these shapes onto your paper, and see what you capture.

2. **TRY A CONTINUOUS BLIND CONTOUR**. Embrace the funky and spontaneous lines that emerge naturally from this drawing style. Start by deciding what you'd like to draw—it can be a leaf, an animal, a building, a landscape, or a friend. Without looking at your paper, draw your subject matter with one continuous line, allowing your pen to flow freely across the page.

3. **DRAW WITH YOUR NONDOMINANT HAND.** This is a wonderful way to let go of habits in order to find a looser, freer way of creating. By inviting your other hand to take the lead, you'll instantly discover new energy in your lines and shapes. Start by drawing something simple and work your way toward more complex compositions as your nondominant hand gets a little practice. Let go and have fun!

THE FIRST NEW MOON OF SUMMER

THE ENCHANTED FOREST

Environmentalist John Muir said it best: "In every walk with nature one receives far more than one seeks." The forest—with its towering trees, rustling leaves, and shrouded veil of mystery—has always served a restorative, spiritual purpose. For fictional characters such as Snow White, Cinderella, and Little Red Riding Hood, fantasy and reality collided in the woods. The backdrop of sacred ceremony, they were honored as a meeting point where the two seemingly separate realms could coexist.

The forest truly speaks to the wisdom in nature, with its mature canopy that has lived through eons, leaves that fall and grow in perfect unison year after year after year, and animals who craft their own habitats in pockets of woods. And while something about the forest is enigmatic and eerie, another part is familiar and comforting. Stepping into the woods can feel a lot like coming home. It's a healing experience spiritually, and, it turns out, physically too.

Bustling cities, smartphones, and distractions have left us overstimulated and stressed, and nature has become an antidote, one whose very presence helps us feel healthier, get closer to our ancestors, and settle back into our bodies. In an age where the average American spends 93 percent of life inside, uninterrupted time surrounded by trees and greenery has been shown to lower heart rate and blood pressure and promote parasympathetic nerve activity (our relaxation response), while calming sympathetic activity (our fight-or-flight response). This is due in part to phytoncides, airborne chemicals emitted by trees that are thought to trigger a healthy immune response in humans.

In Japan in particular, spending time in nature has become a widely accepted form of therapy. The art of *shinrin-yoku*, also known as forest bathing, was coined by the Japanese forestry ministry in 1982. The government then spent millions studying the extensive physical and mental benefits of the practice, and before long, walking on specially designated therapy trails became a legitimate prescription in the country.

The difference between forest bathing and a more commonplace outdoor experience like hiking is the emphasis on journey over destination. Taking a forest bath connotes going out into the woods without a goal in mind and instead just appreciating the experience of being there. It means leaving your map at home and allowing your surroundings to inform your path.

THE JOYS OF NATURE

Perhaps it's no surprise that many of the happiest nations in the world also have programs to help people get outdoors often. In Finland (country #1 on a 2018 World Happiness Ranking), designated forest trails prompt hikers to express gratitude along the way with stone altars, small chapels, and signs that read, "Squat down and touch a plant." In Denmark (#3), *Bofællesskab*—communities with homes built to surround a huge communal garden and green space—are popular, while over in Sweden (#9), a right to nature is literally written in the constitution. *Allemansrätten*, or the freedom to roam, means that citizens can wander anywhere outside, even on private lands. In the reigning happiest city in the United States, Boulder, Colorado, residents voted to put tax dollars toward an expansive three-hundred-mile bike trail around the city, and they recently passed a law saying that every new big building had to be built with either solar panels or a rooftop garden.

A FOREST BATHING RITUAL FOR EXPLORATION

What better way to welcome the first new moon of summer than by checking in with yourself and testing out the therapeutic properties of nature with a forest bathing ritual. Even if you don't have access to an expansive forest where you live, use the occasion to seek out an area that's a little greener than what you're used to. All you'll need is some grass beneath your feet, a view that isn't encumbered by buildings or people, and maybe a chirping bird or two.

WHAT YOU'LL NEED FROM THE OUTSIDE

* Nothing!

WHAT YOU'LL NEED FROM WITHIN

* The readiness to explore your surroundings without a map or phone
  to guide you

INSTRUCTIONS

1. Once you've found your spot, head out without your phone or turn it to airplane mode while you explore. As you go, let the world around you inform your itinerary. Give yourself the freedom to sit on the grass, smell the flowers, maybe dig in the dirt.
2. If you need a little help dropping in and tuning out lingering thoughts or worries, complete a short 1:1 breathing exercise (see page 133).
3. End the experience by taking a snapshot. Your phone and camera should still be put away, so close your eyes and commit the scene to your memory instead by using your senses. What does the moment sound, look, feel, smell, and taste like? Pull up the mental image the next time you're sitting inside and stressed out. It's a reminder of your inherent wildness and of the world, which is bigger than your worries.

There's a reason this ritual is light on instructions. The point of forest bathing is creating your own adventure without stressing about the rules. Going where nature takes you is a spiritual feat in itself.

HOW TO KEEP IT GOING

This doesn't need to be a strictly summertime ritual. There are plenty of techniques for harnessing the brain-boosting, mood-brightening power of nature even when a comfortable midday stroll isn't an option. Here are a few of our favorites:

* Make opening your blinds the first thing you do in the morning.
* Diffuse woody essential oils such as sandalwood, frankincense, and clary sage before bed.
* Grow your own potted herbs on a windowsill.
* Incorporate more houseplants into the spaces where you spend a lot of time.
* Take at least a few minutes outside on the morning of every new moon, when the air is filled with the freshness and possibility that comes at the start of a cycle.

THE FIRST FULL MOON OF SUMMER

DRINK UP THE SUNSHINE

While harnessing flowers for healing is an ancient practice, the term "flower essences" was coined by Dr. Edward Bach, a British surgeon who turned to homeopathy during his own health scare in the 1930s. Frustrated by the limitations of Western medicine, Bach set out to find a remedy in the field that could do more than the vaccines he worked with in the lab. In his quest to find a medicine that could heal the whole person, mind, body, and spirit, he ultimately landed on flowers, thinking that anything infused with the zeal and resilience of nature must be capable of treating man's problems. Once he saw the formulas work wonders in his own medicine cabinet, Bach set out to share them with the masses. He created thirty-eight essences, each one thought to ease a particular emotional distress, from loneliness to fear of the unknown, and detailed their power in his book *The Twelve Healers and Other Remedies.*

In his introduction to the new holistic treatment, he wrote, "As the Herbs heal our fears, our anxieties, our worries, our faults and our failings, it is these we must seek, and then the disease, no matter what it is, will leave us." A bold statement, to be sure, but his assertion that disease can start in the mind has continued to ring true with time. Stress tells the body to release hormones such as cortisol, adrenaline, and norepinephrine, too much of which can leave us overweight and prone to high blood pressure and heart disease.

While there isn't much scientific research supporting the efficacy of drinking flowers, most of us can agree that working more nature into our lives—whether by eating a plant-based diet or spending more time outdoors—can be healing.

Since Bach's time, floral alchemists have stepped forward to craft essences (also known as floral elixirs and flower tinctures) of their own. Today, the market has expanded to welcome bespoke lines of potions that harness

the power of the earth, the sun, and the moon to bring forth a flower for every mood and desire.

A FLOWER ESSENCE RITUAL FOR EXPANSION

It's time to bottle up the energy of the summer's first full moon with a flower essence ritual. Let's conjure up our inner sorceress and create a potion that we can carry with us through the rest of the season.

WHAT YOU'LL NEED FROM THE OUTSIDE

* A small glass spray bottle
* A bowl of water
* Petals of a flower of your choosing

WHAT YOU'LL NEED FROM WITHIN

* An intention to carry forward into the rest of summer.

INSTRUCTIONS

1. On a clear night, head out and place the bowl of water outside under the moon in an area where it won't be disturbed. (If this isn't possible, you can place the bowl on a windowsill to capture the moonlight from inside.)
2. Cover the surface of the water with the petals of a flower that defines summer for you. It could have some sort of memory or story attached; it could have a special meaning in the language of flowers (head back to page 79 to brush up on that); or it could just be one that you find particularly stunning. Choose a flower that is in season and local to your area if possible—and of course, make sure it's one that you're not allergic to. If you can take it from your own garden, even better!
3. As you place each petal in your bowl, play out your summer intention in your mind. Imagine what it would look like to achieve this

seasonal goal, feeling the sensations it would bring you as if they were real. Don't stop until the surface of the water is covered in flowers.

4. Let the bowl sit in the moon overnight and into part of the morning. This way, the sun and the moon can charge your mixture and the intention it holds.

5. Remove the bowl from the sun, strain out the petals, and place the infused water into your glass bottle. Use it as a facial or room mist every morning until it runs out, visualizing your intention again and again with every application.

HOW TO KEEP IT GOING

We asked Katie Hess, the flower alchemist behind the Lotuswei line of essences, to share her top three picks for summertime flowers to infuse and what she loves about each. Bonus: They're all edible and have Katie dreaming of a moonlit picnic in the grass. Jasmine ice cream, a spicy nasturtium salad, and dandelion wine, anyone?

1. JASMINE. Night-blooming jasmine emits a fragrance that envelops the senses. It makes us feel beautiful, full, and whole. It elicits a wildness, a softness, and an appreciation of beauty, both for ourselves and for the world around us.

2. NASTURTIUM. This fiery, red-orange flower is spicy like the hot summer sun! It encourages spontaneity, joy, and contentment.

3. DANDELION. Dandelion dissolves physical tension and helps us melt stress and resistance out of our body. It's wild and free, and its wish-fulfilling seeds blow everywhere, inspiring us to flourish with the wind too.

ꞬNTERNATIONAL KISSING DAY

Ɡ (JULY 6)

SEAL IT WITH A KISS

Also known as World Kiss Day, International Kissing Day came to be in 2006 as an occasion to celebrate lovers. Valentine's Day comes with pressure to perform: the fancy chocolates, dinner reservations, gifts, cards, the whole shebang. Kissing Day, which falls on July 6 every year, is a reminder to simply celebrate love by loving, making it an action-driven holiday rather than a gift-giving one.

These days, kissing is part of many different kinds of relationships. Parents kiss their children, friends kiss on the cheek (sometimes twice), and expressive colleagues even use it as a way to say hello and good-bye in some cultures. There are many guesses as to the origin of kissing: Some scientists say it's an instinctual behavior adapted from when mothers chewed their infants' food before passing it along to them, mouth-to-mouth. Before dismissing that as gross, more recent research shows that kissing may not be as romantic as we think. One international study examined 168 cultures worldwide to see whether kissing played a romantic role. Romantic (or sexual) was defined by lip-to-lip kissing contact that may be prolonged but doesn't have to be. They found that a minority—46 percent—of cultures kissed romantically and that in cultures where romantic kissing cultures were normal, relationships were deemed to be more complex. Go figure.

It may be complicated, but we know when a kiss from a lover or soul mate is special. One of the reasons kissing is so intimate is because the lips are a hot, erogenous zone. When you consider surface area, the lips have more nerve endings than any other body part (even genitals!). Those nerve endings are important for eating, speaking, and, yes, they make kisses feel great. There's something about the shape of your lips together; the movements, energetics, depth, scent, and taste all play a part in whether a kiss is to our liking. In fact, there's an entire science dedicated to the study of kissing—philematology. In an interview with NPR, Sheril Kirshenbaum, the author of *The Science of Kissing*, says that some researchers believe our pheromones decide whether a kissable person makes for a good mate. They're like the body's detective dogs, sniffing out whether our partners are genetically different enough to, theoretically, combine the best of both gene pools to make offspring with fewer diseases and optimal reproductive advantages. Kissing also releases oxytocin, the "cuddling" hormone, in men especially, and helps suppress the production of cortisol, the "stress" hormone, in both partners. Kissing is a conscious action that sends love directly from one's subconscious, animalistic part of the other, and it could help keep couples together.

International Kissing Day is prime time to draw new energy into our lives and to decide whether it's worth keeping. With the help of crystals, which are in some ways like kisses from the earth—each one is unique, and like kissing, they help us manifest chemistry with the people, places, and things by heightening our awareness—we can implement ritual to set intentions that invite the types of relationships and energies we want.

A CRYSTAL RITUAL FOR AN OPEN HEART

Without an open heart, it's impossible to receive the love that's always coming your way. According to Traditional Chinese Medicine, the summer season is correlated with the heart, making it an ideal time to take a closer look at who and how you love. What's preventing you from feeling loved, loving to your fullest, or inviting the kind of love you want into your life?

WHAT YOU'LL NEED FROM THE OUTSIDE

* A candle or palo santo
* Three photos

- One of yourself
- One of someone from a relationship you'd like to repair or improve
- One of someone with whom you'd like to meet or deepen your relationship with. (P.S. None of these photos need to be about romantic love, but they can be.)

* Three pairs of twin tokens (for a total of six). For example, two special coins, two feathers, two sand dollars, two pieces of sea glass, etc. Pro tip: Don't simply choose what's closest. Make it intentional, seasonal, and meaningful.
* Three index cards or similarly sized pieces of paper
* A pen

WHAT YOU'LL NEED FROM WITHIN

* A vision for the role that you want your relationships to play in your life

INSTRUCTIONS

1. At your altar or other sacred space, lay the three photos out before you. Place the photo of yourself on the left, your "repair or improve" photo in the middle, and your "attract or deepen" photo on the right. Have all your twin tokens nearby.
2. Light your candle or palo santo and wave it over the photos to clear the energy around them.
3. Write down a word to represent what's blocking the energy in each or what's been troubling you. There is no wrong answer here, as long as you're honest.
4. Turn over all three cards. On the back of each card, write down a word that you'd like each person to bring into your life, including yourself— let your imagination run wild, but root the final word in reality.
5. Lay a token on each index card. Imagine the tokens absorbing the negative energy from the words on the backs of the cards, much like a crystal would.

6. Lay the other set of tokens on each photo. Imagine the tokens imbuing good vibes, including your chosen words, into each relationship. Think of a scenario in which your chosen word is true and play it out in your mind for each person. This may take a few minutes; don't rush it.

7. Keep these photos on your altar for a few weeks. You can pile them up, turn them over, and rest one of each token on top.

8. Use the other set of tokens as reminders—leave the one for yourself in a place you typically feel lost, overwhelmed, or undervalued. Bring the "repair or improve" token in your bag the next time you see that person. And leave the "attract or deepen" token on your altar or somewhere out in the world where you think it could work to help you manifest that energy.

9. Blow out your candle, stub out your palo santo, and end the ritual by softly closing your eyes and imagining a strong and receptive heart.

HOW TO KEEP IT GOING

If you want to take the ritual deeper or simply keep it going, author and spiritual counsel Emma Mildon gave us recommendations on what types of crystals are most powerful in specific scenarios. Like the power of kissing, using crystals that complement your desires dials up the intensity.

* **CRYSTALS FOR EMOTIONAL SUPPORT.** There are a number of crystals that support your emotions, especially love. Rose quartz is a pink crystal that connects with your heart chakra and is ideal for any matter of the heart: self-love, body love, a healing heart, or simply adding more love into your day. Wear it as a necklace, tuck it in your bra, or add it to your altar. Other stones that are emotionally supportive include amber, green jade, emerald, and garnet.

* **CRYSTALS FOR SEEKING WISDOM.** To harness insight and understanding, enlist crystals that support knowledge and learning.

This includes turquoise, tiger's eye, moonstone, lapis lazuli, and larimar. Keep these crystals with you when you meditate, or hold onto them as you read a new book or digest new wisdom.

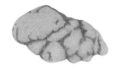

* **CRYSTALS FOR LIFE TRANSITIONS**. Crystals that support us through different life phases, transitions, and the seasons of life can be added to our altars. Azurite welcomes new experiences, onyx brings willpower, and hematite and citrine instill confidence through uncertainty.

A COLORFUL ENERGY

A crystal's color is also thought to say a lot about its energetics. Here are a few common crystal shades and what they mean:

* **Red:** Red stones like rubies carry a loving, passionate energy. The color of blood, red energizes the body and heats us up.

* **Orange and Yellow:** These shades bring about clarity, light, and good fortune, with stones such as amber and citrine acting as portable sunshine.

* **Green:** Green stones are considered extremely healing and grounding. They are often associated with good fortune, with green aventurine and jade being two notable moneymaking stones.

* **Blue:** Blue stones carry a wave of soothing, fluid energy like the ocean and sky they emulate. Blue lace agate and azurite both welcome clarity and make way for loads of creativity.

* **Violet:** Violet is all about spirituality and higher knowing, and stones such as amethyst can help clear one's connection to intuition.

It's interesting to note that some stones—often extremely rare and cherished ones—actually change color based on the light they're exposed to. One example is the tanzanite, which is one thousand times rarer than a diamond and only found in the foothills of Mount Kilimanjaro. It dances between vibrant pinks, blues, and purples. Alexandrite is another gemstone that exhibits many personalities, going from greenish-blue in sunlight to reddish-purple in softer indoor light thanks to its unique combination of minerals.

ꞮNTERNATIONAL DAY OF FRIENDSHIP

σ (JULY 30)

FOREVER FRIENDS

The International Day of Friendship, recognized by the United Nations, is meant to foster camaraderie and strong ties of trust, two fundamental notions brought about by friendship. A "shared spirit of human solidarity," according to the UN, is strong enough to change the world, one true friendship at a time. We wholeheartedly agree.

It makes sense, then, that joy (and its opposite, sorrow) are the emotions associated with summer, according to Traditional Chinese Medicine. Both are emotions experienced in friendships—being vulnerable, hurt, and learning to trust again is part of the process. Naturally, laughter is the sound of summer, per TCM. Think about it—when was the last time you laughed so hard you cried? You were probably with a dear friend.

It's been shown that having solid friendships in childhood and adolescence makes us less self-conscious as adults. Healthy, reciprocated friendship even has the power to offset a lack of support or negative interactions with immediate family members. Hugs from friends have been shown to physically boost our immune systems, suggesting that hugs can actually reduce stress. Even though there have been countless studies quantifying the benefits of real, authentic connections, many of us allow our devices—phones, computers, smart watches, you name it—to do the talking for us. It's true that as a society, we've never been more connected than we are today. And yet, there are also increasing cases of anxiety, depression, and other mental health ailments among people, especially young people—due in large part to the pressure of social media. We can't help but think part of this is because our phones and computers are robbing us of real, in-person connections.

This is one reason yoga has become so popular. It's a chance to disconnect from screens and be in a room with like-minded individuals. Traditionally, yoga is a solitary practice. The word "yoga" is Sanskrit, and in English it translates to "to yoke," "to join," or "to unite." In context of the self, this means the practice of yoga brings the mind, body, and spirit together as one. Having a home practice is satisfying and therapeutic and can certainly achieve this goal on its own. But without a communal practice, we miss out on the chance to share this union with others and benefit from one another's presence.

In Katonah yoga, a newer and more modern lineage of yoga, founder Nevine Michaan maintains that one plus one makes three. The same idea exists in Gestalt psychology—the whole is greater than the sum of its parts. Think of a clap: Joining two hands doesn't make three hands. It makes a new sound. In the same way, practicing yoga with others helps you measure your technique, try new things, and borrow ideas, and ultimately it encourages a collective uplifting spirit.

A PARTNER YOGA RITUAL FOR UNITY

The warmth of the season invites us outside, in the company of new and old friends, to share experiences, wisdom, and stories with one another. Grab a friend—you need only one, but the more the merrier—and complete this yoga flow together.

WHAT YOU'LL NEED FROM THE OUTSIDE

* A yoga mat for each person practicing

WHAT YOU'LL NEED FROM WITHIN

* Openness to collaborate, support, and be supported

INSTRUCTIONS

1. **FIND CENTER.** Starting seated, take a few breaths together to center yourself, ground your body, and notice your mind.

2. **CAT POSE, COW POSES, AND CAULDRON STIRRING.** Moving onto all fours, take a few slow rounds of cats (rounding your back toward the sky, tucking your tail, using your hands to push the floor away from you, navel reaching in and up toward your spine—like a startled cat) and cows (pressing your belly toward the floor, sticking your tail to the sky, raising your gaze, curling the collarbones back) to warm up your spine. Then, make big circles with your hips, a few circles in one direction and then in the other, as if you're stirring a cauldron. Close your eyes if this feels silly, and let it just feel good!

3. **PLANK POSE.** Transitioning into a plank pose, or a pushup position, rock your weight forward and back and side to side, staying for four full breaths total. You should be shaking! If it's too much on your wrists, take the pose on your knees.

4. **DOWNWARD-FACING DOG POSE.** Press up and back to downward-facing dog; your body should make the shape of a triangle with your hips in the sky, and your hands and feet on the ground. Lift your right foot up and back behind you, squaring off your hips. Bend your right knee and open up your hip. Bring your right knee toward your nose, and place your right foot next to your right thumb.

5. **WARRIOR THREE.** From here, spring off your back foot and launch into warrior three. Keep a microbend in your right leg while pressing your left leg back behind you. Flex your foot, square your hips, open your chest, and remember to breathe here. Your head, torso, and left leg should be on the same plane.

6. **STANDING MOUNTAIN POSE.** From here, bend your left leg and come to stand upright on your right foot. Place your left foot next to it for an active break. Stand tall, stacking your bones, with your hands by your sides, facing forward. Take a few breaths here.

7. **DANCER POSE**. Bend your right leg and reach for your inner right foot with your right hand. Instead of using your hand to pull your foot, use your foot and leg to kick into your hand, allowing that motion to lift your leg. Breathe here in dancer's pose, feeling the dynamic movements. When you're ready, release your leg and return to standing mountain pose.

8. **RESET**. Inhale and circle your arms up. Exhale and fold your torso over your legs. Inhale and lift halfway, with your torso parallel to your legs and your hands on your shins. Exhale, fold again. Inhale and ragdoll up to stand, one vertebra at a time, with your head the last to lift. Take a moment here.

9. **REPEAT**. Do the sequence on the other side.

10. **SAVASANA**. After completing the second side, find your way onto your back for a short savasana.

HOW TO KEEP IT GOING

If you want to take your flow to the next level with another person, and you're interested in other ways to support your own practice—and your pals'—giving these adjustments will boost your feelings of connectedness, and receiving them will make you feel supported and grounded. In yoga, like in friendships, the benefits are amplified when we give and receive.

These adjustments are ones you'd typically receive in class from a yoga teacher. Be sure to be gentle with your friends, and engage in hands-on adjustments only if you have consent. You can do these adjustments during the flow just described, helping your partner experience a new version of the postures.

1. **WARRIOR THREE POSE BECOME A WALL**. Standing steadily behind your partner, let her lifted foot press directly into your body. You can also gently hold her foot lifted. Slowly release when she's ready.

2. **DANCER POSE HIGH FIVE**. Standing in front of your partner, bring the palm of your hand in a "high five" shape to meet your partner's hand.

Giving her a wall and a boundary on which to balance will help her stay steady.

3. **STANDING MOUNTAIN POSE ADJUSTMENT.** In standing mountain pose, use your hands to ground her feet. Make an L-shape with your thumb and the rest of your fingers, and hook the space between your thumb and index finger around her heel and traction in toward the ground. This is very calming, grounding, and supportive for the recipient even though it feels like a small gesture.

4. **SAVASANA THIGH BONE ADJUSTMENT**: In final savasana, use your hands to gently press her thigh bones downward into the ground. Mid-thigh usually feels great!

QI XI FESTIVAL

(AUGUST, BUT THE EXACT DATE DEPENDS ON THE YEAR)

A TALE OF LOVE THAT LASTS

Held on the seventh day of the seventh month in the Chinese lunar calendar, Qi Xi, or the Seventh Evening Festival, is the annual meeting of the cowherd and weaver girl in Chinese mythology. The story starts with two lovers, one a skilled weaver and the other a cow herder. They fell in love, married, and had two children. The wife's mother, a goddess, was angered that they were together, so she took her daughter back to the heavens to prevent their union from progressing.

Naturally, the man was distraught and wanted to find a way to be with his wife once again. Soon after, one of his cows revealed a connection to the heavens—he had once been a god too. The man used his cow's skin to make shoes that allowed him to fly to the heavens and be with his wife. All went according to plan, but the queen of the heavens was stubborn. She created the Milky Way in order to keep the lovers apart, but magpies formed a bridge so the lovers could meet in the middle. Seeing how happy this made her daughter, the queen of the heavens allowed these two to be together one day of the year, on Qi Xi. In this way, Qi Xi is now celebrated as a day of romance in China.

There are several rituals performed on Qi Xi. In ancient times women left out fruit and food for Zhi Nu, the wife, and hoped they too could develop a skill, like her weaving, to attract a mate. Children hung flowers on decorative ox horns to honor the cow god who sacrificed himself for the couple. Nowadays, the rituals are different, but all are in the name of love. Paper lanterns are released into the air in Taiwan, and on mainland China some girls hide behind pumpkins to hear the whispers of the couple, which is a good omen for love. Others collect morning dew, said to symbolize the tears of the couple, and wash their hair with it for good luck.

A LOVING–KINDNESS + SOUND HEALING RITUAL FOR ENDURING LOVE

Loving-kindness meditation is traditionally from the Buddhist lineage, but it is used today without any attachment or religious affiliation. Sometimes called the "metta" meditation, the theory of loving-kindness meditation is, you guessed it, to foster love and kindness from within in order to spread and share it with the world at large. Inspired by the undying love of Qi Xi, we will use meditation and sound to invite more love into our lives.

WHAT YOU'LL NEED FROM THE OUTSIDE

* Access to Spotify or another streaming service (This is one time when taking your phone or computer into a ritual is all right.)
* A candle

WHAT YOU'LL NEED FROM WITHIN:

* Compassion and goodwill for yourself and those you come across

INSTRUCTIONS

1. Sit down at your altar or another sacred space and light a candle. Make sure you've found a comfortable seat. Use essential oils here or incense or palo santo if it's helpful in bringing you to the present moment.
2. Set the song "The Oneness Om" by Ananda Giri on repeat. If that's not your jam, search for singing bowls or sound baths without English lyrics.
3. As you sit and take a few deep breaths, imagine what it would look like to send yourself some love. Repeat to yourself: "May you be happy.

May you be healthy. May you be peaceful and live with ease." Absorb that with a few breaths.

4. Next, imagine someone you love so very much. Repeat this to yourself, but send it their way: "May you be happy. May you be healthy. May you be peaceful and live with ease." Absorb that with a few breaths.

5. Next, imagine someone in your mind's eye who is familiar but whom you don't know. This person could be your barista or someone you see on the train every day. Repeat this to yourself, but send it their way: "May you be happy. May you be healthy. May you be peaceful and live with ease." Absorb that with a few breaths.

6. And last, imagine someone you actively dislike. This could be anyone; he or she doesn't have to be in your circle of friends. Repeat this to yourself, but send it their way: "May you be happy. May you be healthy. May you be peaceful and live with ease." Absorb that with a few breaths.

7. Sit with all four people, including yourself, in your consciousness and simply send love to them.

HOW TO KEEP IT GOING

Do a once-weekly sound bath with the intention of connecting inner healing and outer loving-kindness. If public sound baths aren't available in your area, we recommend finding a sound bath YouTube video or purchasing sound healing practitioner Sara Auster's sound bath tracks—these are great because you can upload them to your digital music player of choice and have them ready to go at all times. Sound baths are typically forty-five minutes to an hour long, so set your playlist accordingly. That said, this is your time. Make it ten minutes or longer, but after that, do what's most convenient for you. It's much more important to keep a consistent practice than it is to have a great practice every so often. Here's how it's done:

1. If you're with others, have everyone gather in a circle and lie down so their heads face the center of the circle and their feet extend toward the periphery.

2. Get comfortable—this is very important. Lying on the ground for forty-five minutes is quite bothersome if you're not comfortable. We recommend lying with light head and neck support and a bolster or blanket (or two) rolled up underneath your knees. This will support your back.

3. Set an intention for compassion, and repeat this loving-kindness metta mantra if it resonates: "May you be happy. May you be healthy. May you be peaceful and live with ease."

4. Sit back, let go, and let the sound vibrations work their magic.

5. If you're in a group and feel inclined to do so, share what you felt in a brief circle afterward.

6. If you're bathing solo, take to your journal and write down any inspiring ideas that may have percolated from your subconscious.

Book Lovers Day

(August 9)

THE BIRTH OF THE BOOKWORM

Book Lovers Day, a relatively nascent holiday in the United States, is just what it sounds like: an occasion to celebrate books of all sorts, shapes, and sizes and the readers who bring them to life in their imaginations.

The history of books is as rich as that of language itself. Our first artifacts to resemble books were the clay tablets of Babylon that held legal codes and mathematical texts, and the papyrus scrolls of Egypt that extended a foot in length and followed the dead into their tombs. These early mechanisms immortalized cultural traditions, fables, and theorems. The Greeks were some of the first to recognize the value in studying the texts of other cultures, and they constructed the Library of Alexandria to house them. Intellectuals traveled far and wide with the mission of collecting half a million scrolls to add to their local collections, and the seeds of bookishness were planted.

Back then, libraries were not places of renting and returning. The high cost of production meant books needed to be chained to shelves to prevent theft, and only the rich could afford to keep private collections. Chinese scholars were the ones who ultimately paved the way for modern book culture by creating a way to mass-produce books using wooden blocks that transfer words onto paper. Their language, full of thousands of characters, wasn't attuned to this kind of transcription, though, and it wasn't until German goldsmith Johann Gutenberg introduced movable-type printing in Europe in the 1400s that it really caught on.

From there, books began to come in all shapes and sizes. A Chinese emperor in the fifteenth century ordered the creation of an encyclopedia that sought to collect all the knowledge of mankind. It took more than two thousand scholars to put together, filled more than eleven thousand volumes, and is still considered one of the largest books ever written.

When we hold on to certain old books, it's still possible to feel the love and attention that went into them, to sense the excitement that came from cracking them open for the first time, the frenetic energy that lingers around the end of a dramatic chapter. In that way, reading can feel a lot like transcending time.

A TAROT RITUAL FOR SEAMLESS TRANSITION

Book Lovers Day is an opportunity to appreciate the texts on our shelves and also to expand our horizons to new forms of storytelling. If there was ever a perfect moment to turn to our tarot decks, this is it.

Tarot cards hold their own storied magic and symbolism, and they beg us to start easing into the late summer. While early summer rituals were all about getting out, now it's time to revisit what's within—what's transpired, what's happening now, and all that is to come.

WHAT YOU'LL NEED FROM THE OUTSIDE

* A tarot deck (if you're still looking for the right one, the Golden Thread Tarot app will work too.)
* A journal
* A pen

WHAT YOU'LL NEED FROM WITHIN

* Faith in the cards
* A quiet mind for any intuitive hits to come through

INSTRUCTIONS

1. Light a candle, burn some incense, or do anything else that helps you settle into your space. If this is your first time using your tarot in a while, burn sage over it to metaphorically cleanse it of any energetic gunk that has muddied its cards.
2. Take your deck in your hands and close your eyes. Intuitively choose three cards, laying them out facedown in front of you in a row. The card on the left will represent your past, the middle one your present, the right-hand one your future.
3. Open your eyes and flip each card over. If any are upside down, don't worry—leave them as-is. Look at the cards you pulled and spend a few minutes thinking about what their imagery means for you before consulting a tarot deck guide. Pull out a journal and write down the words that come to mind when you look at each. Then, spend some time placing them in the context of your life. How do these words speak to

your past, present, and future? Even if they seem totally foreign, what messages can you glean from them? Spend a few minutes ruminating on these questions with nothing but your intuition to guide you before you look up what tarot language has to say about your pull.

4. Refer to the booklet that comes with your deck to look up what it says about each card. Biddy Tarot is also a good resource if you're looking for more detailed descriptions. Complete your journaling exercise by adding any relevant words or phrases you find there. Pay special attention to the future card. What does it say for the rest of your season and year?

5. If you feel called to do so, carry the future card you pulled around with you for the rest of summer—place it in your wallet, in your purse, or on your desk or nightstand—as a reminder of the larger forces at play.

HOW TO KEEP IT GOING

Lindsay Mack, tarot reader and founder of Wild Soul Healing, offers a couple of her favorite three-card spreads that you can turn to for guidance whenever you need it.

A CHECK-IN FOR THE SOUL SPREAD
    Card 1: Present moment
    Card 2: Subconscious
    Card 3: What I'm being invited to pay attention to

This spread is perfect for getting clear on the larger world and our inner world; macrocosm and microcosm. It can help us to check in with our soul's highest purpose and with what we are being invited to pay attention to at this moment.

DROP INTO THE PRESENCE SPREAD
    Card 1: How can I be more present with myself?
    Card 2: How can I be more present with my loved ones?
    Card 3: How can I be more present with the world around me?

This is a beautiful spread, one that can identify how we can be present, not only with ourselves and our loved ones, but also with the world around us. The more we drop into this kind of presence, the quicker we can become agents for change on this planet, our home.

Ιnternational Day of Peace

☌ (September 21)

The United Nations designated September 21 the International Day of Peace in 1981. The occasion is a global observation of peace meant to unify all of humanity. Every year, citizens of countries around the world come together to celebrate the fact that despite our differences, we are all living on the same Earth. Though a dove holding an olive branch is the official symbol of this holiday, we like to think of peace as the trees in a forest: a collection of organisms standing strong next to one another, providing tranquil habitat for all creatures.

Trees are a lot like us. For one, they embody all the elements: They have roots that extend deep into the earth and branches that reach high enough to kiss the sky. They drink up water and become fuel for fire. Surprisingly enough, trees are also incredibly smart and adaptable, able to emit less appealing resins when critters chomp at their leaves. And their abilities are not strictly self-serving. Trees are nurturing, social creatures, able to communicate with one another through a network of fungi buried beneath the soil. Ecologist Suzanne Simard likens forests to a single organism, tied together by seemingly infinite biological pathways below the ground. To this end, trees also possess a maternal instinct, able to recognize their own seedlings and send more care their way, and they can reroute their own root system to make way for their offspring. In fact, a mother tree is able to give life to hundreds of other trees at once.

Though human in their behavior, many trees outlive even the oldest of us. The Methuselah in California's Inyo National Forest—which roughly translates to "dwelling place of the great spirit"—dates back 5,066 years, and in Sweden, Old Tjikko—named after its discoverer's dog—has been growing for an incredible 9,550 years. Methuselah is knotted and bare, and Old Tjikko resembles a discarded Christmas tree—although gnarled in appearance, they possess sage wisdom.

The sixty thousand species of trees in the world all come with stories attached. From the fruit-bearing tree that tempted Adam and Eve to the apple tree that helped Sir Isaac Newton find gravity, humankind's journey has been irrevocably intertwined with the trees. Through time, we have also counted on trees as time markers and sacred secret keepers. During the two years Anne Frank spent in hiding, she turned to the chestnut tree visible outside her window as a symbol of freedom and perseverance. "Our chestnut tree is in full bloom. It's covered with leaves and is even more beautiful than last year," she wrote in her diary. Hordes of chestnut saplings have since been donated to schools and other organizations in her name. European legend says that it's impossible to tell a lie under a linden tree, so judicial hearings were once held under their cover. Hunters used to depend on the sounds of the forest for clues about their prey, and indigenous cultures still look to trees for guidance of the spiritual sort. Some even claim to have heard the trees sing.

We all climb their trunks as children and turn to their cover for shade as adults. We look to their leaves as colorful signs of the seasons, but we also chop them down and turn them into paper to hold our ideas. We take their sap to sweeten our lives and destroy forests in our quest to grow more food. Our relationship with trees may be complex, but one thing is for certain: Trees deserve our respect and, even if just for today, our emulation.

A ROOTING RITUAL FOR SOLIDARITY

It's fitting that the International Day of Peace occurs when the leaves of the trees are just beginning to change color in the northern hemisphere. This last ritual of summer will call on you to epitomize the sage, supportive, and—yes—peaceful energy of trees as you move forward into fall.

WHAT YOU'LL NEED FROM THE OUTSIDE

* Nothing!

* A willingness to stand still and look a little silly in the name of strength for a few minutes

INSTRUCTIONS

1. Find a place outdoors to stand barefoot on the earth, preferably one with a few trees in sight for inspiration.
2. Take on the form of the official solar system symbol for planet Earth (a circle intersected with a plus sign, split up into four sections to represent the four elements of earth, water, air, and fire) by extending your arms to either side of you. In doing so, you'll also emulate the shape of a tree, with its branches stretching outward.
3. While you may feel a bit silly standing in this position, stay with it as you slow down your breath. With your first few inhales, imagine that the energy of the earth is coming forth from the ground, feeding you and filling you with life as it does for the trees that surround you. With each following breath, visualize this strong, steady, supportive energy slowly moving farther up your body, your trunk.
4. Once this energy reaches your chest, imagine it spreading outward to your arms. Once it reaches your hands, see it emanating out of you and into the greater world. You are the keeper of loving earth energy, and it is your job as a human to spread it to others.

Let this quick, simple visualization remind you of your capacity to inspire change in those around you by tapping into the power you already hold within.

HOW TO KEEP IT GOING

At its core, ritual work is not self-serving. By slowing down and getting quiet with yourself, you're increasing your capacity to help others. We can take this a step further by carrying through with rituals with the sole purpose of helping the people and places around us. Here are a few more outward-facing rituals to carry in your back pocket moving forward:

1. **START A PRESENT—GIVING RITUAL.** Make the last Friday of the month a day you pick up a small trinket for someone you care about, and impart it with a wish for that person before you present it to them.
2. **INFUSE YOUR DINNERS WITH MORE GRATITUDE.** Every season, organize a dinner gathering with some friends and complete the night by going around the table and sharing one thing you love about someone else at the table. Continue until each person has spoken of everyone else.
3. **CHOOSE A CLEANUP DAY.** Make a weekly ritual of cleaning your neighborhood as you would your home, even if for just a few minutes. Complete a meditation afterward, silently thanking Mama Earth for all she has given you.

Autumn

*It was a beautiful bright autumn day, with air like cider
and a sky so blue you could drown in it.*
—Diana Gabaldon, *Outlander*

AUTUMN IS A POWERFUL TIME OF TRANSITION. Beginning with the full ripeness of summer and ending on the shortest day of the year, fall asks us to recognize the fruits of our labor, enjoy them, and then turn inward. Unlike the steady building energy of summer and winter, autumn is a consistent decrescendo. A display of fiery foliage is Mother Nature's way of showing that even the most beautiful things aren't permanent—it's a performance of her final number before she releases it all and retires till spring.

As forest animals collect enough nourishment for a season of hibernation and migratory birds soar the skies toward warmer destinations, we gather around food and toast to the year as the weather gets colder. Abandoning the ease and joy of summer can leave us feeling anxious as we begin to clear the slate for the long winter ahead. On the home front, the start of fall is prime time to finish long-term projects and tie up loose ends before heading into winter's reflective abyss.

CAUTUMN: A HISTORY

Autumn is historically and presently harvest season in northern areas of the world. Ancient cultures have celebrated the harvest with festivals for as long as we have record. While Thanksgiving is often viewed as an American holiday, many cultures around the world see gratitude and family gathering as an essential component of their harvest rituals.

China and Vietnam, for example, have a moon festival, also called the mid-autumn festival, that falls midway through the eighth lunar cycle—on the full moon—and is celebrated by admiring the moon with friends and family, reciting poetry, and eating moon cakes. If lovers are separated on this holiday, they give each other a call and gaze at the moon simultaneously.

In Japan, Ohigan marks the start of both autumn and spring. Not to be confused with Shunbun no Hi, the day of the Japanese spring equinox, Ohigan is a weeklong period that extends three days before and three days after the spring and autumnal equinoxes, for a total of seven days. Named for a flower that blooms in autumn, Ohigan is a Buddhist tradition of meditation and quiet, one in which the Japanese honor those who have passed by visiting their burial sites, cleaning them up, and decorating them. The word "Ohigan" itself has roots in Sanskrit and means "reaching Nirvana."

Thousands of years ago, native Iroquois women living in present-day America would make dolls to give "the spirit of the grain" a place to live after the harvest, when corn and other grains wilted and died. These dolls were made from corn husks, using corn silk for the hair, and helped ensure the success of the following year's harvest. In other traditions, corn husk dolls were made after the harvest, given to children as toys in an effort to use every part of the corn.

The ancient Greeks have their own explanation for fall and winter. If you recall from spring (page 96), the Greek goddess Persephone's return to her mother, Demeter, led to a flourishing landscape. In the fall, when Persephone returns to the underworld—still bound by her deal with Hades—Demeter's sorrow becomes so great and all-encompassing, it drains life from the earth as well.

Perhaps one of the more magical elements of the fall (and spring) equinox is the aurora borealis. This stellar phenomenon can be seen from the northernmost slice of the northern hemisphere in countries such as Denmark, Canada, Iceland, Greenland, Norway, and even some parts of the United States. The spectacular display of colors is a result of the earth's atmospheric geomagnetic storms, which occur twice as often in the spring and fall as they do in the summer and winter. What better way to tune in than through a show that reminds us we are all stardust?

THE SEASON'S SIGNIFICANCE

In Traditional Chinese Medicine, the season of fall is marked by grief, worry, and sorrow, and it corresponds to the lungs. Home of the breath, the only automatic, organ-based body process we can also actively control with our minds (unlike digestion, for example), the lungs make fall a special season indeed. When we take a deep breath, we're well ventilated. And this openness can help us experience fall's heavy emotions with support from the union of our mind and our body. We can use the airways to make space not only in our bodies, minds, and hearts but also in our lives. On the other hand, fall is a time when the respiratory system is newly taxed with chilly air and autumnal allergens (hello, ragweed), making us more susceptible to catching an airborne illness.

In Ayurveda—a slightly different language that marries earthly elements to bodily constitutions—autumn carries a *vata* energy. *Vata* is the combination of air and space. Someone who has a strong *vata* energy is said to be light, often cold, nervous, capricious, and irregular. Needless to say, grounding practices are needed to help balance this anxiousness.

MODERN AUTUMN RITUAL

Current fall celebrations honor the bounty of the harvest. Smaller moments such as apple picking, sipping hot cider, and admiring the fall foliage, along with arguably the biggest feast of the year, Thanksgiving, bring together people of all belief backgrounds and walks of life for a meal. It's not a coincidence that many food-focused holidays happen as the days get shorter and chillier. These rituals remind us that we're not alone, even though the dark and cold can make even the peppiest of optimists feel that way.

With the enormous commercial emphasis on Halloween, the modern celebration has lost its meaning. For this reason, we chose to focus on All Saints Day for a ritual—not because of religious affiliations or preferences but because it's important that modern ritual feel sacred.

AUTUMN IS A TIME TO . . .

✳ Celebrate the harvest by giving thanks to Mother Earth.

✳ Enjoy nature's gifts of fall foliage, meteor showers, and aurora borealis.

✳ Swap lighter fare for energy-producing root vegetables, grains, and hearty greens.

✳ Balance *vata* energy with grounding practices.

✳ Drink warming herbal teas to clarify your lungs.

✳ Finish long-term projects to make space for reflection and exploration.

✳ Breathe deeply to help your body and mind transition into the quiet space of winter.

The rituals of fall embody the season's duality. Anytime we experience a substantial amount of outer change—moving from the freedom of summer schedules to more structure, the temperature dipping, and the landscape evolving, to name a few—it's too easy to underestimate the inner shifts that occur as a result. The truth is that they happen whether we're aware of them or not, and if they're left out of balance for too long, it'll manifest in illness or unwelcome change.

By honoring these earthly and bodily shifts using ritual, the mind and body will be primed to handle the transition with grace and ease.

THE AUTUMNAL EQUINOX

TASTE THE RAINBOW

On the autumnal (and vernal) equinox, the amount of sunshine and darkness is exactly the same. Each day gets shorter by the minute until the short-

est day of the year—the winter solstice. As we slip into days that are more dark than light, it's important to remember that autumn is an intersection of celebration and release.

And the celebration comes first! Our senses are delighted with the sights, tastes, and smells of the earth's bounty. Traditional Chinese Medicine calls us to enjoy the last of summer's fruit at the start of autumn for their cleansing properties. Mid-season is a time of indulgence in colorful, healthy, nutrient-dense foods such as squash, beetroot, and sweet potatoes. As temperatures plunge outside, Ayurvedic wisdom tells us to eat warming foods: soups, chilis, stews, and hot apple cider, to heat us up from the inside. Warming spices such as cinnamon and nutmeg remind us of the holiday celebrations to come. Believe it or not, garlic is a powerful healing herb that works well with the energy of autumn, according to TCM. Taken internally, it's been known to help restore mucus membranes in the nose, mouth, and lungs, fending off colds and respiratory infections.

Many of fall's harvest-centric holidays, as jovial as they are at first, also require an element of letting go. In order to celebrate Mother Earth's bounty with a seasonal feast, we have to pluck it from the vines, ending the cycle of fertility for the year. Fall starts with togetherness and ends in solitude. Magnificent foliage becomes bare branches as leaves fall. Instead of huddling around a campfire under the stars, people gather around a fireplace indoors. The energy of the season entices us inward.

A HARVEST RITUAL FOR ABUNDANCE

For farmers, autumn's harvest season means taking stock of what grew this year. Throughout the season, they have to assess what's ripe enough to pick, what to leave for later, and what to let go of until next year.

The timeline of our lives mimics this energy: Fall brings a burst of activity and then a feeling of settling in and hunkering down. It's a time to take inventory. What has come to fruition, and what hasn't? What seeds do you wish you had planted, in hindsight? What have you nurtured to full maturity, and what did you neglect? With this ritual, you will take a moment to contemplate these questions and celebrate the harvest of your life.

WHAT YOU'LL NEED FROM THE OUTSIDE

* Physical objects that remind you of your achievements
* An altar or other special place to display them
* A pen
* Paper

WHAT YOU'LL NEED FROM WITHIN

* A mental (or physical) list of all you've accomplished this year

INSTRUCTIONS

1. Grab your pen and paper, and sit near your altar or settle somewhere comfortable, quiet, and indoors where you can be uninterrupted for fifteen to twenty minutes.
2. Spend some time thinking about and jotting down your most notable moments this year. Reflect on your intentions from January and see what came to fruition or what you happily released. Also notice if any unsolicited good came your way. It could be anything: a moving book you read, a memorable night out, a well-deserved promotion, finally

saying no to someone—jot down anything that made you feel great, right, or sure. Don't worry about putting them in any particular order yet.

3. From this list, narrow down your moments to the five that make you feel most aligned with who you want to be.

4. Using your edited selection, gather five objects that remind you of these moments and place them on your altar or somewhere they can be prominently displayed. This is your harvest—whether these came from goals you set or came your way without solicitation.

5. Practice receiving and understanding that what you have in front of you is enough. Know that especially now, the season of fall supports abundance. Accept it with grace.

HOW TO KEEP IT GOING

Judy Choix is a New York State Licensed Mental Health Counselor (LMHC) trained in Gestalt and body psychotherapy, as well as the founder of Full Gestalt. Believing that the body holds the wisdom to heal itself, her practice

combines talk therapy with energy work to facilitate awareness around malfunctioning energy patterns both in the body and the mind.

Celebrating your own personal harvest can be more difficult than it seems. In fact, many of us have trouble receiving and feeling as if what we've done in a year is enough. We spoke to Judy about the practice of grounding and how it can energetically, and eventually physically, lead to a shift in how we interact with the world.

Energy has a natural structure that, when supported well, is connected and flowing. We get disconnected or dysregulated when we spend too much time in our heads, on our tech, or engaging in other destructive patterns. Grounding is a practice that can help promote better habits and prevent falling into old patterns. Benefits of grounding include enhanced mental and emotional clarity, reduction of stress, and a general feeling of well-being. In my experience, a consistent daily practice will not only regulate the system, it will also revitalize your energies!

The following meditation will take about twenty to thirty minutes and can be performed either seated or standing, indoors or outdoors. Find a quiet space, and experiment with what works best for you. In my practice, I've seen that the effects of this work are cumulative—which means the more you repeat this exercise, the stronger and more immediate your results can be.

1. Sitting or standing upright, find a place in which your spine is erect and the soles of your feet are "rooted" in the earth (so sitting in a chair is preferred to sitting cross-legged). This posture allows your energies to flow. Make sure you are comfortable.

2. Closing your eyes, place one hand on your heart and the other on your low belly. Breathe through your nose slowly and deeply. Feel your stomach expand as you inhale and relax as you exhale. Do this for a couple of minutes until it becomes rhythmic and effortless. As you engage the diaphragm by breathing into your belly, envision tension being released from all your muscles. Notice how you feel.

3. Starting from the crown of your head, bring attention to your head, face, throat, chest, arms, and downward until you have "touched" all your parts with your mind's eye. Invite your energies in these areas to descend until your attention is on your feet.

4. Imagine that your feet grow roots that extend down toward the center of the earth, passing easefully through concrete, bedrock, and more.

5. When you get to the center of the earth, a red hook forms at the end of these roots and grabs onto the center of the earth. You are solidly held and supported here. Feel that nothing can knock you over. Imagine you are like a tree, free to bend with the wind but lovingly rooted and supported.

6. Begin identifying anything that is not supportive or needed in your life. Let these energies leave your body while you're tethered to the earth. Let go of anxiety, judgment, and anger. Take as long as you need to flush out these excess energies. Notice how you feel.

7. When you're ready to come out, do so slowly, knowing that this grounding is with you and available to you wherever you go.

THE FIRST NEW MOON OF AUTUMN

TAKE A BREATHER

The seasons of the year mimic the cycle of the breath. Winter is a hold on empty, spring is an inhale, summer is a full, pregnant pause, and fall is an exhale.

During this season, leaves fall, heavy fruits and veggies are harvested, and the air crisps, quite literally cueing us to exhale and let go in preparation for winter. Metaphorically, then, autumn calls us to recognize our most significant achievements and transitions. It asks us to tie up loose ends on anything still pending and then let it go. If winter is a time of deep contemplation of what we want from this life, fall is a clearing, albeit a complex one, to move into winter with a lighter load and a more spacious mind. As mentioned before, the lungs play a huge role in fall, and one of the most effective ways to let go of stagnant energy is with the almighty breath.

In Traditional Chinese Medicine, the lungs and the large intestine are the organs associated with autumn. As temperatures decline, people are especially prone to coming down with colds, respiratory infections, and allergies—but maintaining your self-care and health care are ways to keep the lungs in top shape. Interestingly, along with the large intestine, skin, and kidneys, lungs are an elimination organ; they help rid the body of carbon dioxide, toxins, and pathogens.

Skull-shining, or *kapalabhati*, breath is a way to move stagnation, aerate the lungs, and bring newfound clarity to a foggy mind. It's a powerful and detoxifying breath exercise. *Kapalabhati* is a series of short, sharp exhales through the nose that activate the diaphragm. On the inhale, the belly relaxes and expands, and on the exhale, the abdomen snaps in toward the spine to force the air out. Yogis believe that this breath is cleansing for the body and the mind, oxygenating the blood, massaging internal organs, and releasing held stress. In that way, it's the perfect complement to the release of harvest season.

While the term *kapalabhati* is often used interchangeably with "breath of fire," they're not the same. The exhale in *kapalabhati* is longer than the inhale, and the inhale is passive. In breath of fire, the breaths are both the same length, and the inhale is more active.

A BREATHWORK RITUAL FOR BIG SHIFTS AND CHANGE

The new moon symbolizes new beginnings, and in the context of harvest season, it invites you to tie up loose ends, complete projects, and ready yourself for the restoration of the colder months. All this considered, autumn's first new moon is a powerful time to pair breathwork with intention.

If you're new to breathwork, feel free to experiment and take this one slowly. Also, if you're pregnant, think you might be pregnant, are on the first few days of your cycle, or just ate a giant meal, refrain from this exercise. Instead, just breathe deeply through this ritual and follow along.

WHAT YOU'LL NEED FROM THE OUTSIDE

* A comfortable place to sit (including props such as a block, blanket, or chair)
* A white article of clothing
* Your journal
* Your favorite writing utensil

WHAT YOU'LL NEED FROM WITHIN

* The ability to stay focused
* Respect for your own boundaries
* Preparedness to release what doesn't serve you

INSTRUCTIONS

1. Wear something white. Not only is white the color of autumn according to TCM, it symbolizes purity, radiance, and reset. In the

Kundalini yoga tradition, Yogi Bhajan, one of its prominent teachers, said that wearing white can increase your radiant auric field by at least one foot. We'll take it.

2. Find a comfortable seat on a block or blanket, cross-legged, in hero's pose, or seated in a chair. *Kapalabhati* is stimulating, so be sure you can relax and feel supported wherever you are. If you feel dizzy, light-headed, or out of breath at any time, feel free to take a break and pick back up whenever you're ready.

3. Think of three things in your life that no longer serve you. Like falling leaves, release what you no longer need. Write these down in your journal before you begin your breathwork.

4. Inhale through your nose, allowing your belly to expand. Exhale, letting the breath tumble out the mouth. Do this two more times to prepare.

5. Place your hands palms down on your thighs, a sign of grounding. Inhale about halfway, and forcefully push the breath out of your nose by snapping in your navel. Try it a few times before you really get going. With your focus on short, sharp exhales, your inhale should flow without effort or thought.

6. Once you get the hang of it, do two rounds of thirty short, sharp exhales, taking a breath in between. On your last breath of each round, inhale fully, bringing your hands above your head in prayer. Hold for three seconds, take three more sips of air through your mouth, and exhale, letting the breath tumble out of your nose while you bring your hands back to the tops of your thighs, palms facing up, a sign of receptivity.

7. After two rounds of *kapalabhati*, breathe normally for a minute, returning to your natural state. Notice any shifts: How do your mind and body feel different? Write down any visions, insights, thoughts (no good or bad here), or anything from the experience that you'd like to release.

This exercise is an excellent example of our powerful ability to create our own realities. It takes only a moment to shift our energy. While you're breathing, know that you're moving stagnation through the body. You might feel tingly, light-headed, or a little dizzy. That's normal. Feel free to take a moment to breathe normally and then return to the practice.

HOW TO KEEP IT GOING

If you're interested in starting or improving your breathing practice, breathwork teacher Ashley Neese describes her three top tips and tricks to help you stick to it.

1. **START WHERE YOU ARE.** When it comes to breathwork, it's normal in the beginning to worry if you are doing it right. Here are some simple suggestions to help ease your mind and get you practicing:
   * Find a comfortable place to practice with as few distractions as possible.
   * Set a timer for five minutes.
   * Bring your awareness to your breath and breathe slowly in and out through your nose.
   * When you're ready, begin the specific breathwork technique you are exploring.
   * As you become aware of your thoughts, gently come back to your breathwork.
   * When the timer goes off, close your practice by thinking of one thing you are grateful for.

2. **SLOW DOWN.** It's always best to start slow and build a breathwork practice gradually. There is no need to rush because our practice evolves as we do and will continue to grow over time. To set yourself up for success, even with more activating practices such as *kapalabhati*, it is wise to set a pace that doesn't overwhelm your system and builds heat and energy over a series of practice rounds. Repeat your practice a couple of times a week, working your way into a daily practice. When you miss a day or two, be gentle with yourself and simply begin again.

3. **PRACTICE CONSISTENTLY.** Once you get into your practice rhythm, carve out the time for it each day. The most potent benefits of breathwork arise from dedicated practice over time. When done consistently, breathwork can boost mental clarity, recalibrate the nervous system, and stabilize emotions. It's amazing how much you can learn about yourself from committing to a regular practice.

THE FIRST FULL MOON OF AUTUMN

HARVEST THE LIGHT

The full harvest moon falls in September or October, whichever is closer to the autumnal equinox. Different from any other full moon, the moonrise of a harvest moon happens rapidly after the sun sets, keeping the sky well lit on a clear night. (Normally, once the sun sets, a full moon takes approximately fifty minutes to rise, but a harvest moon takes only thirty minutes or less to rise, for several nights in a row.) Historically, before farmers had access to electricity, the flood of moonlight allowed them to stay out in the fields collecting the season's harvest. That's how the moon got its name. It seems insignificant, but when the daylight hours are few and far between, the extra light is a big help.

According to astronomers, a harvest moon happens because the ecliptic—a fancy name for the imaginary line in the solar system that tracks the orbit of the sun, moon, and Earth—creates a shallow angle at dusk. The northernmost latitudes in the northern hemisphere will see the moon rise even faster, at fifteen minutes, while the effect is minimized for southern locales.

Full moons, those that arrive in autumn in particular, are opportunities to release what is no longer serving you. And the simple act of humming can help you do so. Yep, humming is a simple way to self-soothe with sound. It can change your energetic state from frenzied, scattered, or stressed—as it is prone to be in fall—and bring it back to a healthy baseline.

GOOD VIBRATIONS

There's a growing body of scientific evidence that proves the restorative potential of sound, underscoring the fact that our voices are an underutilized healing tool. A review by Harvard Medical School found that the vibrations of music help people re-cover more quickly after invasive surgery, improve the quality of life for people with dementia, ease pain, and allow stroke and cancer patients to heal faster. Older re-search also shows the healing power of vibrational frequencies for patients with fibro-myalgia, who were able to withstand more physical pressure on weak points than their placebo-controlled counterparts. Open-heart surgery patients who received physio-acoustic therapy (low-vibrational frequencies) after surgery required less medica-tion, spent fewer days recovering, and didn't need the ventilator as much as patients who didn't receive vibrations. When people hum together, the neurons in our brains actually sync more than when we sing together.

There's even a theory that humming first arose to maintain mother-infant at-tachment, nodding at its limitless potency and potential to soothe. Other academic texts theorize that the sound of humming is in fact creative energy manifested.

Since humming has proven so comforting to the nervous system, giving it a try during a stressful situation—a Monday morning commute, right before a big presen-tation, or any other time you feel overwhelmed—can help ground you.

If you think it's a little strange to hum out loud when you're alone, or in front of others, know you're not the only one. A large part of self-care is get-ting to know yourself by doing things that might be out of your comfort zone, noticing how you react, and having the compassion to not immedi-ately judge yourself. If you feel silly (we all do at times), remember it's tem-porary and for the sake of deeper healing.

A HUMMING RITUAL FOR TUNING IN

If you have a hard time listening to your intuition, making your own sound is a helpful way to tap into yourself when everything else feels loud. We can use humming as a tool to move from the doing mind into the receiv-ing or practicing mind and to open to the energy of the full moon. Let's dive into a humming ritual to help you find clarity with the help of the night's bright sky.

WHAT YOU'LL NEED FROM THE OUTSIDE

* A comfy place to sit
* Loose, comfortable clothing

WHAT YOU'LL NEED FROM WITHIN

* A receptive heart
* The courage to hear yourself and your own sound

INSTRUCTIONS

1. Find a quiet place where you can get comfortable and sit uninterrupted for about five minutes. This ritual is effective but efficient.
2. Imagine yourself in your mind's eye, and then begin to deconstruct that image. What colors, scents, temperatures, textures, and other qualities are you made of? Are you oceanic or made of desert, or flowers?
3. Feel out how the image in your mind's eye is different from where you want to be next year. This can help you determine what you'd like to manifest by next year and clarify what's needed to get there.
4. Now that you've brainstormed, clearly imagine the qualities needed. If you decided fire was your element, feel the heat. If mint was your flavor, taste and smell it. If you wanted to manifest abundance, perhaps you chose green as a color. Pick three to five qualities to focus on and hold in your senses.
5. Sitting for a moment, allow one of these elements to come forward. Instead of choosing it, let it choose you. Listen to what wants to be heard.
6. With a singular, clear point of focus, seal your lips and take a deep breath in and exhale through your nose. Do this a couple of times.
7. On your next inhale, engage your low belly and start to hum. Hum into your colors, smells, tastes, and textures. This will help you trans-

late the sound and find your frequency. Don't be afraid to play if it's not right at first.

8. Once you've found your frequency, take a few rounds of belly breaths and begin to hum once more.

9. To seal the practice, continue imagining and hone in on a singular point of focus. Find a crystal or other symbolic object and charge it on your windowsill with the energy of tonight's harvest moon. Let it be a reminder of your desired reality and the person you want to become.

Regardless of what you sound like, do your best to refrain from judgment, to remove your ego from the exercise, and allow your body to begin to heal itself.

HOW TO KEEP IT GOING

Sound healer and sound bath facilitator Sara Auster is one of the world's most in-demand sound healers, leading sound trainings and immersions all over the globe. Here, she shares a four-step deep-listening technique you can use to tune in using ambient noise.

1. **CLOSE YOUR EYES AND LISTEN.** See if you can notice the sounds both in the room and outside the room. Some might annoy you at first or not be particularly pleasant, but draw your awareness to them. Allow and accept the sounds as they are. If you've opted to include music or the sound of any instruments like singing bowls or a gong, focus on the sound and the contrast it leaves in the room after it fades away.

2. **STAY LOOSELY FOCUSED ON YOUR BREATHING.** Let the sound be a secondary focus of the practice. Call to mind the creators of these sounds and embrace the sound as part of your practice.

3. **BECOME AWARE OF THE SPACE AROUND YOU.** Become conscious of the space in front, behind, and to the sides—even above and below you. Allow yourself to feel as if your mind is expanding into the surrounding space and even expanding outside the room.

4. **LET THE SOUNDS YOU HEAR ANCHOR YOU IN THE PRESENT MOMENT.**
   Try not to get caught up in judging what you hear or analyzing the sounds; just listen, observe, and experience them. If you become restless or impatient, acknowledge these feelings but do not react to them. Stick with this for at least five minutes and see how your awareness has shifted from the beginning of the practice into a calmer, more relaxed state.

Make a difference day
(October 28)

SAY IT OUT LOUD

A mantra is a string of sounds—syllables, single words, or a phrase—that's sacred and powerful.

It has been suggested that mantras are even older than language itself. Something so ancient is bound to have a rich, conflicted history, but most sources maintain that the oldest known mantra stemmed from Vedic meditations by Indian Hindus, originating more than three thousand years ago. Today, mantras are used across many religions in worship, yoga practice, and ritualistic ceremony to alter consciousness and enter the nonthinking mind, where present-moment awareness lives.

There isn't as much published research on mantras specifically as there is on meditation. But mantras and meditation used together have been shown to decrease blood pressure in patients with hypertension, suggesting that the duo could be just as powerful as medication in some cases.

Common mantras taught in meditation today include "om," "soham," "shanti," and "sat nam." One of the major conflicts in mantra philosophy is meaning. Have you ever experienced the phenomenon in which, after saying a word over and over again, it begins to lose its meaning? There's a term for that: semantic satiation, semantic saturation, or verbal satiation. It facilitates a state of mindful focus, where you can sit in present-moment awareness and enjoy the sound of your mantra without getting caught up in its meaning. Most experienced teachers and practitioners insist that you not inquire into the meaning of your mantra, as doing so can interfere with its purpose of bringing you back to the present moment.

THE MEANING OF MANTRA

Om: Pronounced *a-u-m*, om is said to be the universal, languageless sound. When it's chanted, it sounds more like "ah," "oh," or "mmm" than "om." The "a" stands for the waking state, and the sound comes from the belly and back of the throat. The "u" stands for the dream state, and it resonates in the soft upper palate of the mouth. The "m" vibrates through the lips and nose and stands for the state of deep sleep.

Soham: In Sanskrit, "so" means "I am," and "ham" means "he" or "that," which refers to the the big, the divine. When used in meditation, this mantra is meant to connect you with the universe. It can be chanted or linked to the inhale (on "so") and exhale (on "ham," which sounds like "hum").

Shanti: Shanti is Sanskrit for peace and is often chanted at the end of a yoga practice or as part of a longer prayer. "Shanti, shanti, shanti" is a prayer for peace.

Sat Nam: This mantra stems from Kundalini yoga. "Sat" stands for "true," and "nam" stands for "name," which can translate to true essence. Saying sat nam to another is a nod to the divine within.

In some traditions, such as Transcendental Meditation, your teacher whispers a mantra into your ear that's yours and yours alone. In order to practice it, you need to receive it from a teacher. While this has proven effective for many, many people, we believe there's more than one way to find a mantra. Consider this personal story from Lindsay:

For as long as I can remember, I was triggered by mantras I'd see on Instagram, hanging on the walls of yoga studios and coffee shops, and written in self-help books.

"You are beautiful."

"You are enough."

"You are perfect."

I couldn't put my finger on what the big deal was. What invisible force was keeping me from getting on board here? If these phrases were empowering women I looked up to, why weren't they working for me? These questions played in the background of my life—which, as a wellness editor and yogi, is rife with mantras—for quite a while.

Someone close to me suggested it was because I needed to hear these mantras myself and had my own work to do around it. I agreed—of course! Obviously, I said. Anyone with a regular practice knows there's always a new stone to turn, and I'll be the first to admit I'm a work in progress. It wasn't that—no matter how many times I explored how they resonated with me, these mantras still felt inauthentic.

At the same time this quandary surfaced, I struggled to keep a regular meditation practice. I couldn't sit still the way I used to. There was always a phone to pick up, a feed to scroll through, a to-do list to tend to, a more "productive" way to spend alone time, or something urgent that needed my attention. Sitting was always last. While working out one morning (ahem, still not sitting still . . .), I asked myself: Why can't you sit still on your own, without guidance from another? I couldn't answer it at the moment, but I knew that I'd be able to examine this the next time I had a chance to meditate.

Later that day, the chance arose. I had a good twenty minutes to sit. I reached for my phone and caught myself: Why aren't you sitting? Then, it came: Historically, my biggest block was that I wasn't qualified enough to have my own practice. But now I'm a yoga teacher, with training in restorative yoga, meditation, breathwork, and self-inquiry. . . . There goes that excuse. Why else aren't you sitting? Here's the aha moment! It was because when I sat, I felt trapped. I had nowhere to go and had to entertain myself.

Scrolling through Instagram, which is what I would do instead of sitting, you can run, run, run down any hole until the next distraction needs your attention. Or you can answer emails for hours on end. You can distract yourself by shopping, eating, reading, listening to podcasts, even moving—any kind of consuming. And just like that, there it was. By way of consumption, I thought I was finding freedom. In reality, I was chasing it like the good old carrot dangling from a stick.

The same trapped feeling often happened when I sat down to write long-form or to create. Given the sheer number of books, articles, and essays written about creative blocks, productivity, and how to get things done, it's safe to say that a fear of sitting with ourselves and our thoughts is pretty common. It happens even in situations we choose to be in! Next time you find your mind wandering (or your thumb scrolling), ask yourself why you're not here, now.

In order to tease myself out of avoidance and into the present moment, I came up with, yes, a personal mantra: "In this moment, I am free." Whenever I found myself avoiding something that I knew I was capable of, whether it was work, a hard conversation, or a meditation, I reminded myself of my freedom. The aforementioned affirmations didn't feel authentic because they didn't ring true with my narrative. In order for a personal mantra to resonate, it can't be forced.

AN AFFIRMATION RITUAL FOR EMPOWERMENT

Today marks Make a Difference Day, a national day of service in the United States. Let's use it as a cue to tackle some of our less productive habits using mantras, so we can walk out into the world better equipped to help others.

In modern wellness slang, the word "mantra" has also come to mean one's own personal catchphrase, crossing over into affirmation territory. Both are powerful and important, and this ritual will reveal how to design a personal mantra that feels empowering and authentic.

WHAT YOU'LL NEED FROM THE OUTSIDE

* A habit you want to change

WHAT YOU'LL NEED FROM WITHIN

* Softness of heart and mind that allows you to peel back a layer

INSTRUCTIONS

1. Identify a behavior you don't like that's keeping you from doing something you desire. Once you flag it, plant this idea: Next time this happens, I will pause.
2. The next time it comes up, you pause. Notice, and ask yourself what you're trying to do by engaging it. What are you avoiding? (Chances are you know, deep down.) That will be the foundation for your own mantra.
3. Once you think about what you're avoiding with this behavior, begin to consider what you are chasing with it. I was avoiding sitting with my own thoughts and believed I was chasing freedom. Ask yourself whether it's true. For example, in my case, would I find freedom in going out to buy another latte? Or another sweater? Where do you find what you're looking for, really?
4. After your brief inquiry, form the base of your own personal mantra with what you desire. Then add to it with what you know to be true. Mine was freedom: I wanted to remind myself that I choose to meditate and that I am free in that moment. So I came up with "In this moment, I am free," which reminded me that, even when I don't feel free, I still have agency over my choices.

Write down your mantra somewhere, and don't forget it. Revisit and tweak it as you see fit. It's yours and yours to keep!

HOW TO KEEP IT GOING

So many moments, like repeating mantras, can become meditative. But there's a difference between being meditative and meditating. As we see it, meditation is an active state that involves pruning the inner landscape and building our increasingly fractured attention. Here are a couple of meditation techniques that work well with mantra. Test them out to see if they're a fit for your personal rituals and routines as well.

* **TRATAKA MEDITATION.** If you need a little extra help focusing, this one is for you. Trataka means "gaze" in Sanskrit. This meditation is typically done by gazing at a candle for an extended period of time without blinking. Try three minutes or less to start, and do your best not to blink. When three minutes is up, close your eyes and imagine the object in your mind's eye. Technically you can do this with any object, but the flame of a candle is traditionally used. If you have cataracts, glaucoma, myopia, astigmatism, or epilepsy, don't do trataka.

* **MINDFULNESS MEDITATION.** This labeling tool is excellent for beginners but is practiced by experienced practitioners too. Mindfulness meditation starts with a simple awareness of breath—this can be your entire meditation. If you're feeling antsy, try watching the thoughts as they inevitably whir past your consciousness. You are witness to those thoughts, not engaging them. Once you're comfortable with this (if you're brand-new to meditation, it might take a few sits), move into the next phase: thought labeling. As thoughts come up, put them into broad-stroke categories, such as "work," "relationships," "creativity," "money," "home," "family," etc. These are just examples, as the categories will be different for everyone. This technique is designed to give you information on the things occupying your mind. It's advanced because it's not meant to feel like effort.

$\mathcal{S}$AMHAIN

$\mathcal{G}$ (October 31–November 1)

GOING FULL CIRCLE

Around this time of year, it's said that the veil between earthly life and the afterlife is at its thinnest. It's no wonder that Samhain, Halloween, Day of the Dead, and All Saints Day—occasions rooted in celebrating and honoring

those who have passed—fall within a few days of one another in autumn. If communicating with the dead sounds appealing, the end of October and the beginning of November is a good time to try it.

Día de los Muertos is a Mexican celebration that extends three days, from October 31 to November 2. Adults and children make altars, visit the tombs of loved ones who have passed away with offerings of sweets and food, and celebrate them with meals, parades, and gatherings. All Saints Day, which falls on November 1, is a Christian holiday to celebrate all passed saints with a feast in their honor. Then, there's Halloween, which actually comes to us by way of Samhain (pronounced "SAH-win"). Samhain originated from Gaelic tradition and historically signified the start of winter and the end of the harvest season.

Samhain was an occasion rich with ritual. Since people really believed that spirits came to visit during this time, extra precautions were taken:

People wore their clothes inside out and carried salt to ward off unwanted spirits, or they simply stayed near home and avoided going out alone in the dark. At dinner, families made table settings for the dead to visit and played games. In fact, Halloween's bobbing for apples tradition was born from Samhain, as apples were associated with the spirit realm and immortality. Then there was the Samhain staple of "mumming and guising," which gave rise to trick-or-treating. Back then, people would dress up in costume and go from house to house singing or speaking songs in exchange for offerings meant for spirits. Sound familiar? Other Samhain rituals included divination, which is considered the oldest form of magic. Guided by the energy of spirits who could see into the future, people would predict major life events, such as death and marriage, during this time.

A MANDALA RITUAL FOR GUIDANCE

Talking about death, dying, and the dead—let alone communing with them—is still largely considered taboo today. But this time of year offers a beautiful opportunity to connect with any loved ones who have passed for guidance about a current question, conundrum, or direction if you're feeling lost. By accessing the divine creator within yourself through a mandala practice, you just might be able to tap into otherworldly planes to channel their energy and, if desired, their presence.

When communing with the dead, it's common to feel like a lack of closure leaves you with too much to say. But your mandala—which translates to "circle" in Sanskrit—can serve as a physical reminder of the intention you set and the questions you want to ask.

WHAT YOU'LL NEED FROM THE OUTSIDE

* A protective crystal, such as black onyx, amethyst, or smoky quartz
* A pencil
* A compass or anything around your home with a circular base (like a mug)
* A ruler or straightedge

* Paper
* A fine-point marker or a thick-line pen (feel free to use varying widths if that's your thing)
* Colored markers, pencils, crayons, or paints

WHAT YOU'LL NEED FROM WITHIN

* A willingness and strength to feel energy of spirit
* Mindfulness to set aside any need for perfection

INSTRUCTIONS

1. Find a place where you can sit quietly, uninterrupted, for at least an hour. Light a candle, clear your table, and set your supplies out in front of you.

2. Put your crystal on a blank page and call in any spirits you'd like to commune with. Call them by name, tell them your intention, share your question, and ask for guidance where you need it. When you're finished, move the crystal away to begin the mandala.

3. Using your compass, mug, or other household items, draw as many concentric circles (circles around the same center) on the paper as you wish in pencil, and as large or small as you wish. We suggest you go with the flow instead of measuring here. Perhaps even choose a number with significance to you or the spirits you're channeling.

4. From here, use your ruler and pencil to draw four lines in pencil. Start by dividing the circle into half, then quarters, then eighths, and finally sixteenths. Each section should be about the same width. (If it's not, your mandala will be asymmetrical, which is A-OK!)

5. Starting at the center, draw patterns within each concentric circle, using the lines of each section as guidelines. If you're comfortable, start with pen; otherwise, you can always trace over pencil marks later. Choose a pattern that's symbolic or one that feels good to phys-

ically draw. The shapes can take up one or two sections, depending on how you want the scale to look.

6. Do about a third of your circle, and then add a pattern (if desired) to your designs. Then draw another third of designs, adding another pattern to those. Patterns are a great place to experiment with lines, dots, shading, and intricate details. Feel free to use different pen thicknesses and line weights here.

7. Use these designs as a way to add significance to your work, but don't think too much. Allow yourself to get lost in the repetition.

8. When you're happy with where you've landed, adding color and pattern, erase your pencil marks and add color within the lines. Allow it to mean something to you. You can do this all at once or take a break and come back to it every day, coloring one ring at a time until they're all done.

9. Once you've finished, place the crystal back on the mandala and blow out your candle. Thank your spirit guides for the energy they supplied you while making this mandala, and know it will serve as a reminder of them. Keep it wherever you need a reminder that you're always guided and never alone.

HOW TO KEEP IT GOING

We spoke to Ally Bogard, a yoga teacher, meditation guide, and spiritual counsel, about the notion that each one of us has a "spiritual council" of our own. Here, she gives us background and advice on how to get in touch, activate, and commune with them peacefully.

We can't always see, believe, or even imagine a benevolent, loving, and intelligent council of beings who care for us, who want good for us, and who are here for us—just as we are here for them. But it is a beautiful relationship to build. Trust and intimacy between you and your ancestors, spirit guides, animal allies, forces of nature, angels and archangels, masters, teachers, and the highest "I Am" presence with yourself can be an awe-inspiring and encouraging connection. You can call on your spirit council for support, clarity, direction, guidance, and help pointing your inner compass to be in the right place at the right time for your highest fulfillment.

To create a connection with your council, it is helpful to suspend the notion "I'll believe it when I see it," and instead open up your mind to a place where "I'll see it when I believe it" is true. Here is an exercise to get you started:

1. This practice begins with your eyes open. Sit quietly, or lie down in nature. Whatever you are looking at in your field of vision, truly see it. See the way light and shadow shape form. Let the sound of traffic or the rustle of leaves feel like vibrations in your inner ear, and let it ripple through your body. Use your sense organs to feel alive now, through sensation.

2. As you relax into your surroundings, orchestrate the feeling of abundant, life-fulfilling support that is always available to you by appreciating the simple and otherwise overlooked things that make your life possible. This includes oxygen, food, water, love, guidance, and natural forces that are always working to provide you with ample opportunities to live a vibrant life.

3. Take a moment to let your entire body bathe in appreciation for how truly supported you are. Imagine yourself being surrounded by light and love and unconditional support.

4. In the energy of relaxed appreciation, close your eyes. If there is someone who has passed to the other side whom you specifically wish to bring forth, ask permission for their soul to be invited into your field. You have protection from the pure light of *the One*. Or, call upon other allies, angelic forces, animal spirits, and benevolent guides in alignment with the source energy you have cultivated.

5. Take a few silent moments in appreciation or prayer, or request specific guidance or signs from your council. Thank them for their presence in your life.

6. To seal the practice, sit quietly and simply feel. As you open your eyes and go about your day, do your best to stay in curiosity. The way in which your council speaks to you will be unique. They may use music, numbers, book passages, technology, messages from friends, etc. The important thing is to suspend disbelief and watch for the symbolic world to speak to you. Translation of the messages and their timing is best received with an open and grateful mind.

11/11 (NOVEMBER 11)

ONE ON ONE

For many, 11:11 is a time to make a wish—a lucky moment that falls a cut above the rest. This superstition is rooted in numerology—the study of how numbers can serve a spiritual purpose and play into our life's path.

Repeating numbers (or Master Numbers) in particular are thought to signal a higher force—spiritual guides, guardian angels, God, whatever you acknowledge—working to get your attention. Each repeating number means something a little different, and 11:11 is especially transcendent. That's because the number 1 speaks to new beginnings in numerology, and four of them standing side by side creates the illusion of two doors. Some intuitive healers believe that one door represents the earthly realm; the other, the spirit realm. This is a visual symbol of the veil between the two worlds lifting, allowing us to dance between them as we wish. Therefore, 11/11 can be a day to zoom out and really examine if your earthly actions are in alignment with your higher purpose. According to numerologist Michelle Buchanan, it's a day to spend quality time alone by contemplating, meditating in nature, or doing yoga.

While some people may scoff at the idea that certain dates hold energy, many others have signed on to it. One wedding service reporting that 24,900 American couples got married on 11/11/11, compared to just 1,700 on other Fridays in November. (Walt Disney World was sure to cut off the number of weddings it hosted on that date at—you guessed it—11.)

A TALISMAN CRAFTING RITUAL FOR GOOD LUCK

This ritual will encapsulate the powerful spiritual energy of the number 1 into a talisman that you can carry forward into the rest of the year.

WHAT YOU'LL NEED FROM THE OUTSIDE

* A bell
* A charm, bead, or trinket
* A jewelry-size chain

WHAT YOU'LL NEED FROM WITHIN

* An intention you'd like to carry into the next season
* Some craftiness

INSTRUCTIONS

1. Take the single trinket you chose and place it on your chain to make a necklace. It can be any object: a shell, an infinity symbol, a coin. Feel free to add other adornments to your talisman.
2. Once you fashion your necklace, hold it in one hand, close your eyes, and think on one of the spirit-driven goals that you identified in the past year or a previous ritual. Today is an especially potent day to will it to come true, since it signals the move between two doorways and two realms of consciousness.
3. Still holding on to your talisman, start to visualize what it would be like if you brought this intention to life. Open your palm to reveal the talisman, and begin ringing your bell over it. Many cultures consider the sound of a bell an analogy for angels and spirit. Along with numbers, music is the other element thought to signal the presence of a higher power.
4. Once you have programmed your talisman with intention, and with a little help from the spirit realm, wear it or carry it with you as a charm that carries the good luck of 11/11.

Winter is an especially inward-facing, spiritual time, so this little trinket will come in handy as you transition.

HOW TO KEEP IT GOING

We asked numerologist Michelle Buchanan about another date that comes packed with meaning: Friday the 13th. Here's what she had to say:

In numerology, the number 13 is known as a "karmic debt number." Therefore the thirteenth day of any month (no matter what weekday it falls on) signals a time to work hard and put in the extra effort required to accomplish your goals. This is a day to be extra focused, organized, determined, and persistent.

Patience, perseverance, and an optimistic attitude are the keys to getting through the day. You may experience frustrations, obstacles, or delays when the next Friday the 13th comes around, but if you focus on the end result, things will eventually fall into place.

World Kindness Day

(November 13)

KINDNESS IS CONTAGIOUS

World Kindness Day actually arose out of nastiness. One day in 1960s Japan, Mr. Seiji Kaya, the president of a university in Tokyo, was mugged on a train as passersby looked on without stepping in to help. Disappointed, Seiji Kaya went on to promote a kinder culture around the city, starting in his school. He told his students that small acts of generosity could build into something greater, saying, "I want you all to be brave in practicing small kindness, thereby creating a wave of kindness that will someday wash over all of Japanese society." Year after year, this wave slowly took form, building the energy and momentum to become a global movement. In 1997, World Kindness Day was designated a global holiday—an occasion to remember how rewarding it is to put others before ourselves.

Participating member nations include the United States, Canada, much of Europe, India, China, and Brazil. Kindness looks a little different in each one. In Singapore, flash dance mobs break out in the streets come November 13, and yellow daisies are passed out to symbolize innocence, purity, and beauty and send kindness "blossoming" around the city. In Australia, residents are encouraged to register a "kindness card" online when they see someone completing a nice action, and these cards can turn into a heartwarming collection to be shared on the holiday. In the United States, kindness may be a stranger buying you a coffee, holding a door open for you, or simply smiling in your direction.

Leading up to the holiday's twentieth anniversary, member countries gathered to discuss how kindness can contribute to a healthier, happier society. The ways are plenty, and though it may sound too corny to be true, the simple act of doing something for others can improve your own well-being. Studies show that, on average, people who carry through acts of kindness, such as donating to charity or buying someone flowers, feel happier and more satisfied with their lives. They also tend to see the world as a better place, which forms a positive feedback loop of sorts: The more often you act with kindness, the better your world seems. And the brighter your world, the more you feel called to be kind right back to it.

A REFLECTION RITUAL FOR SELF-LOVE

While today is all about being kind to those around you, let's also use it as a chance to turn some of that positivity inward. With this ritual, you'll pay yourself the compliments you'd usually reserve for others in a thoughtful display of self-love. After all, you need to tend to your own flame before you can step out into the world to pass your light on to others.

WHAT YOU'LL NEED FROM THE OUTSIDE

* A pen
* Paper
* Scissors
* A metal jar (or any container with a lid)

WHAT YOU'LL NEED FROM WITHIN

* Permission to pay yourself a compliment

INSTRUCTIONS

1. Sit down in front of your fall altar, or in a special space, and think about what you love about yourself. Turning to the harvest you've gathered for inspiration, talk to yourself as you would a friend or loved one. Begin by paying yourself compliments, without feeling as though you need to follow them up with a "but." What quality traits have helped you land where you are today?

2. Commit these words of encouragement to the page. Write them down in large print and cut them into little slips—like fortunes—when you've filled a full page. Keep going until you run out of things to say.

3. Fold up all the affirmations and place them in your metal jar. Metal is the element of fall in Traditional Chinese Medicine, celebrated for its ability to change shape. It is a strong, rigid material that becomes liquid and malleable when exposed to heat. We can all use some more of this nimble energy in our lives. Let your jar be a place to let go—of the need to be perfect, of the tendency to be too hard on yourself, of the desire to downplay your accomplishments. Instead, just appreciate what already is. Allow yourself to be soft and hard at the same time.

4. Leave the jar on your altar and pull a slip from it any time you're having a bad day. Let it serve as a reminder of all that you are already giving to the world.

HOW TO KEEP IT GOING

We spoke to Natalie Kuhn, executive director and founding teacher of the Class by Taryn Toomey, about how to undo patterns of negative self-talk. While teaching the Class by Taryn Toomey, Natalie helps people reprogram their inner dialogues through physical fatigue and emotional awareness. Here's a ritual based on her teaching.

1. The first step to breaking up with the negative voice in your head is to tune in to that voice—let it ring through your mind loud and clear, and remind yourself that this voice is not *you*. Most of our waking lives are spent living on autopilot with a constant internal monologue—without anyone actually listening! So the first step is to notice it. "Huh; I'm telling myself I'm too old/too young/too skinny/too dumb/too unqualified/too fat/too uncool/too [fill in the blank]. Interesting. There's that voice. Good to know."

2. Put on your favorite song that's got some soul to it. (For me, it's anything by Alabama Shakes, Mumford and Sons, or A Tribe Called Red.)

3. Turn it *up*. All the way up.

4. Repeat one movement for the duration of this song. It could be running, if you have access to the outdoors, or a repetitive movement like jumping jacks if you're at home.

5. As you begin to move on the beat, allow that thought—that voice that lends itself to destruction rather than to support—to come up. Then, with a fierce curiosity, examine it. Is it fact or fiction? What caused you to start saying it? How often have you said it? What's the feeling underneath it?

6. Now *use* your body to express it, whether it's frustration that you've been saying that thing for far too long, sadness that you've begun to identify with it, or anger that you've given your time and energy to it. Use the movement, the beat, the melody to express the thought fully through your body. You might sweat, cry, laugh, make sound. Do what you need to do in order to feel it fully. And keep on it for the duration of the song.

7. At the end of the song, place your hands on heart and drop your breath into your belly. Close your eyes. Feel the shift. Remind yourself that you are not your thoughts. You are not at the mercy of your thoughts. You are the unlimited energy *behind* your thoughts. You are the creator of the voice in your head, and you have the power to change that voice. As our founder, Taryn Toomey, always says, "You have everything you need: You've got you."

THANKSGIVING

☙ (FOURTH THURSDAY OF NOVEMBER)

SHARING IS CARING

Thanksgiving is thought of as an American holiday, but the act of looking back on the seasons and the cycle of the harvest can be applied to any culture, religion, or group of people. Mother Earth provides a bounty, and we are all thankful to consume it.

That said, the history and origin of this holiday hold a special meaning for Americans. In the seventeenth century, shortly after settlers from England arrived on the *Mayflower*, the Wampanoag tribe helped settlers learn to fish, farm, and hunt local game. Squanto, a Patuxet Indian who knew English, taught them about the land and how to get on with the Wampanoag. (This remained one of the only peaceful moments between the Native Americans and settlers, which is why many people across the country refuse to celebrate traditionally—in protest of the way Native Americans were treated by American settlers.) They used this knowledge to procure a prolific feast that lasted three days, according to some records.

For many years the tradition continued as an informal gathering of settlers and Native Americans. It took more than two hundred years to mark Thanksgiving as a federal holiday. Several states celebrated it on their own (fun fact: New York was the first state to make it official) before Abraham Lincoln officially declared it a holiday during the Civil War in 1863, in order to "heal the wounds of the nation," he said.

Historically speaking, honoring the harvest with a big meal is standard fare. The Greeks, Romans, and Egyptians celebrated goddesses of fertility with a feast, and it's said that Native Americans may have even had their own harvest supper in place before the settlers arrived. But according to its origin story, American Thanksgiving was more about healing and sharing among cultures than it was about the feast.

A GROUNDING REIKI—INSPIRED RITUAL FOR HEALING

When thinking about how to honor these themes of healing and togetherness with modern ritual, Reiki immediately comes to mind. Reiki is a form of "alternative" healing that's said to move energy through the body. Technically speaking, in order to do Reiki, you need to have an attunement—a training session with a Reiki master in which he or she transfers the Reiki to you. The idea is that all Reiki comes from one master and has been transferred. Once you have it, you bring it with you everywhere and can eventually attune others too.

Reiki master Kelsey Patel maintains that "we are all Reiki. Each one of us has this healing potential and connection available to us inside." That's to say you don't necessarily need a Reiki session to experience the healing power of its touch. Nonsexual touch can be medicinal in itself when we're healing each other. Receiving it from others moves energy through the body in a way we can't always do for ourselves, removing blocks and decreasing stagnation. While not much medical research has been done on Reiki as a healing modality, we do know that it's used in leading hospitals throughout the country.

In this partner ritual, you'll be guided through a healing grounding session based on Reiki principles. Try it out with a loved one before Thanksgiving dinner to see what sort of energy you can dig up pre-turkey.

WHAT YOU'LL NEED FROM THE OUTSIDE

* A yoga mat
* Permission to touch your partner
* A candle or a stick of palo santo to burn, if desired

WHAT YOU'LL NEED FROM WITHIN

* Loving-kindness
* A mind-set that readies you to give and receive

INSTRUCTIONS

1. Set up your yoga mat and light your candle or palo santo.
2. Ask your partner to stand at the center of the mat in *tadasana*, mountain pose, and ask for her consent to touch. As you prepare to heal, think about being love, feeling love, and emitting love and kindness.
3. Sitting behind her, make an L-shape with your fingers; your thumb is the bottom and the four fingers are on the side, like "Barbie hands." Slide your hands around the bottom of her heels and direct them toward the ground firmly but gently. Stay here for a few breaths.
4. Then work up to her hips. Now standing, narrow her hip points together. Using the same hand positioning, squeeze gently but firmly and pull slightly down. Stay here for a moment. When you release the pressure, keep your hands there for a few breaths before moving on.
5. Bring your hands to her shoulders and, palms facing down, intentionally place them there. Don't allow your hands to go slack or rest. Imagine transferring energy that allows your friend to grow roots and feel grounded. Stay here for at least a minute.
6. Take your hands to her occipital lobe, which is close to where the hairline and neck meet on her head. With both thumbs pointing down in the center and your fingers fanning out around her ears, use your thumbs to gently press in and pull upward. (If your friend is taller than you, have her get into a comfortable seat for this one.)
7. Finally, bring your right hand to the crown of her head and gently tap it with your ring and middle fingers for twenty to thirty seconds. This moves the energy up and out of her head.

Repeat the sequence in the opposite order, going back down to her shoulders, hips, and feet. Then, if your partner is game, switch spots to receive some healing magic.

HOW TO KEEP IT GOING

We talked to Kelsey Patel, a Reiki master, to get some more background on Reiki and snag her favorite self-healing touch ritual that can be completed solo.

Reiki uses directed universal life-force energy to achieve healing on all levels of our being, including physical, emotional, mental, and spiritual. It works with whatever you, the healer, or the recipient (the other person, place, or thing) needs in the moment for the highest good.

The Reiki precepts are codes of conduct that Usui Sensei, the founder of Reiki, believed were the art of living a happy life and were medicine to the soul:

> Just for today do not worry;
> Just for today do not anger;
> Just for today be humble;
> Just for today be honest;
> Just for today be compassionate toward yourself and others.

The intention of this exercise is to bring about harmony and align your body's left and right hemispheres with breath. As you do this, you also balance the left and right sides of your brain. It is best for anxiety, exhaustion, depletion, mental stress, and any feelings of imbalance in your mind or body.

1. To begin, sit in a cross-legged position and lengthen your spine.
2. Take your right hand across your chest and place it underneath your left armpit, releasing your thumb to rest on the front of your left shoulder.
3. Now, take your left arm across your chest and place it under your right armpit and release your thumb to rest on the front of your right shoulder.
4. Begin breathing. Take a few breaths by inhaling through your nose and exhaling through your mouth; then transition to breathe in and

out of your nose. You may immediately feel the imbalance between the left and right sides of your body, and that's okay.

5. Continue to breathe in for a count of three, and breathe out for a count of three to four. Relax your shoulders and the rest of your body while you breathe. Do this for three to five minutes and simply focus on your breath.

6. Allow the inhale to bring in clarity and the exhale to let go of stress or anxiety.

7. Once you complete the exercise, release your hands and remain seated for a few breaths to feel your body and mind coming into harmony and balance. You may also want to set a prayer or intention for the rest of your day or evening that connects you to a feeling of balance and harmony.

ᒪETTER WRITING DAY

ᕖ (DECEMBER 7)

DEAR DIARY

The first written spell, traced back to an ancient Middle Eastern civilization called Sumer, kicked off the practice of eliciting magic and sorcery through words.

Many cultures placed a lot of power in the written word, as showcased by artifacts like the twenty-page illustrated Egyptian book of spells, which had recipes for everything from banishing evil spirits to finding love, gaining power, and treating disease. In Egypt, doctors would also prescribe spells as a means of treatment, while belief systems like the Japanese *kotodama* say that words and names hold mystical force.

In 1801, the English occultist Francis Barrett summed up the potency of language in saying, "The virtue of man's words are so great

that, when pronounced with a fervent consistence of the mind, they are able to subvert Nature, to cause earthquakes, storms, and tempests. . . . Almost all charms are impotent without words." What an idea: that, depending on how they're used, words can be vehicles for miracles.

We believe that writing a letter is one of the most powerful ways to release your words to the universe. Writing is a divine communication, and even if you don't send it, a heartfelt letter is heard by someone, somewhere.

A WRITING RITUAL FOR PRESENCE

Before we start to transition into winter once again, let's wrap up fall with a ritual to celebrate Letter Writing Day in America, an extremely straightforward holiday that calls on people to write letters to those they care about. Our ritual will ask you to find words for all that you want to welcome with the next season and beyond. Instead of crafting a note for someone else, though, you'll be addressing it to yourself.

WHAT YOU'LL NEED FROM THE OUTSIDE

* A pen
* Paper
* A candle or incense

WHAT YOU'LL NEED FROM WITHIN

* An openness to whatever your spirit really wants, regardless of whether it aligns with your "plan"

INSTRUCTIONS

1. Light a candle or incense to tell the mind it's time to slow down. Sit in a comfortable position and close your eyes.
2. Use a few deep breaths to drop in, and then begin to visualize yourself standing at a large wooden door. You knock on the door and find that the person on the other side of it is also you—five years from now. Your future self ushers you into a room. Everything about this room feels right: the decor, the light, but mostly the woman standing

in it. Your future self is strong and powerful, and she speaks with ease about all that she has welcomed into her life recently and all that she plans to soon. What is she saying? Listen without judgment and really let anything come through, no matter how silly or unfamiliar what she is saying may seem. Finish the visualization by thanking your future self for her openness on your way out of the room.

3. Immediately after you open your eyes, take your pen and begin writing a letter to the woman you just met. Recount what she told you, congratulate her on her achievements, and wish her luck through the next phase. Don't worry about grammar or syntax—make it a quick and free-form letter. Think of your words as an extension of the visualization, separate from ego or rational mind.

4. Finish the ritual by signing the letter, folding it up, and placing it in an envelope to set on your altar—the first relic to welcome winter.

Moving into the most inward-facing season of all, this exercise will give you some insight into all that you want to work toward manifesting in the coming months.

HOW TO KEEP IT GOING

Julia Cameron, the original authority on helping creative people get unstuck and unblocked, offers four tips on how to break through blocks as they (inevitably) arise. These tips are from Julia, as told to Lindsay.

"The biggest drain of creative energy is what I would call perfectionism. People don't want to start something unless they can do it perfectly, so they are stymied and don't start. But if you're willing to do it badly, give it a try. People feel a sense of freedom, then they try."

1. **MORNING PAGES**. Julia's first and seminal book, *The Artist's Way*, was the first of its kind to break major ground among creatives who were stuck and among people who didn't think they were creative but were. Morning pages require three pages of longhand, and must be done first thing upon waking. Set aside some time to write

freely in the morning—grammar, punctuation, and rules no longer apply.

2. **A SOLO ARTIST DATE ONCE A WEEK.** Take yourself out to do something fun. Assigned play leads to the play of ideas—which don't come as readily if you're always putting your nose to the grindstone. Go out! Have some fun, and learn something new.

3. **WALKING.** When people walk, they integrate the insights they've received from morning pages, solo artist dates, and memoir writing.

"When you work the tools, you become in touch with a 'benevolent something.' You can call it the universe, Spirit, God, or Tao. It's a benevolent force working on our own behalf. We become aware of this force when we work with the tools, and we become able to risk more because we feel we have a net."

EPILOGUE

There will come a time when you believe everything is
finished; that will be the beginning.
—Louis L'Amour

FOR EMMA, ritual looks a lot like a run along New York City's West Side Highway. It's the steady breathing, the repetitive movement, the chance to tune out worry and be grateful for the city that surrounds and the body that allows her to explore it. It's a journaling practice at the start of every moon cycle. A moment to sit in bed and let the pen write something that nobody else will ever read. For Lindsay, it's a consistent yoga practice, the only long-term constant in her life other than writing. It's using her physical body to access emotion, shift energy, and give this otherworldly soul a terrestrial home. It's a restorative ten-minute moving meditation at the end of every day. It's returning to the mat and the page over and over again, even after longer-than-intended lapses.

Through these rituals, we get to access the spirit in ourselves, and we are forever grateful for the clarity, support, and love it provides. They give us tools that help us to see life with curiosity, love, and beauty even when it gets difficult. We hope that this book has helped you discover and hone rituals that do the same for you.

May this be part of your beginning.

With spirit,
Emma & Lindsay

ᏗCKNOWLEDGMENTS

We'd like to thank Charlotte Edey for bringing the rituals to life through her striking interpretations—without her, this book wouldn't be nearly as beautiful.

Thank you to our brilliant and open-minded editors, Sara and Heather, for being so receptive to our thoughts, ideas, and wishes throughout not just the writing process, but all the logistics.

Amy, thank you for believing in the book that could.

Many thanks to our colleagues Elle, Leigh, Bobb, Gretch, and Liz for the daily encouragement and amusement.

Thank you to Aaron, for taking care of nearly everything while I sat down to write, and thank you Mac, for the late-night company. Many thanks to Sherry, Stuart, Rachel, Mark, Sasha, and Dan for understanding missed dinners. Thank you to Kimi, Lauren, Jessie, Melissa, and Amanda, whose daily texts and encouragement meant more than you'll ever know.

Thanks to Phil and June—and Pip!—for your smiles and support.

Endless gratitude to the experts cited in this book, and the ones we have learned so much from, for sharing your stories, your passions, and your love with us: Dr. Eva Selhub, Christopher Satch, Tanya Carroll Richardson, Jennifer Racioppi, Anjie Cho, Alexandra Roxo, Ruby Warrington, Paula Mallis, Britta Plug, Kumi Sawyers, Jenn Tardif, Dages Juvelier Keates, the Sky Ting family, Robin Rose Bennett, Jessa Blades, Ramesh Tarun Narine, Natalia Hailes, Ashley Spivak, Flora Bowley, Katie Hess, Emma Mildon, Lindsay Mack, Ashley Neese, Sara Auster, Kelsey Patel, Julia Cameron, and Michelle Buchanan. And a very special thanks to Judy Choix and Ally Bogard, whose sound counsel laid the groundwork for the energy that infused this book.

Finally, thank you for the miracle that is our Mother Earth, to source energy, to our animal allies, spirit guides, and all that is.

APPENDIX

GET TO KNOW OUR EXPERTS

Dr. Eva Selhub—www.drselhub.com
Christopher Satch—www.thesill.com
Tanya Carroll Richardson—
tanyarichardson.com
Jennifer Racioppi—jenniferracioppi
.com
Anjie Cho—www.anjiecho.com
Alexandra Roxo—www
.alexandraroxo.com
Ruby Warrington—www
.rubywarrington.com
Paula Mallis—paulamallis.com
Britta Plug—brittabeauty.com
Kumi Sawyers—www.skytingyoga
.com/kumi-sawyers
Jenn Tardif—www.jenntardifyoga
.com

Dages Juvelier Keates—www
.dagesjuvelierkeates.com
Robin Rose Bennett—www
.robinrosebennett.com
Jessa Blades—www.jessablades.com
Ramesh Tarun Narine—rameshtarun
.com
Natalia Hailes and Ashley Spivak—
www.ourbrilliantbodies.com
Flora Bowley—florabowley.com
Katie Hess—www.lotuswei.com
Emma Mildon—www.emmamildon
.com
Lindsay Mack—www.lindsaymack
.com
Judy Choix—www.fullgestalt.com
/index.html
Ashley Neese—ashleyneese.com
Sara Auster—saraauster.com
Ally Bogard—allybogard.com

Kelsey Patel—www.kelseyjpatel.com
Julia Cameron—juliacameronlive.com
Michelle Buchanan—www
.michellebuchanan.co.nz

SHOP AROUND

The Alchemist's Kitchen—www
.thealchemistskitchen.com
Stick Stone & Bone—www
.stickstonebone.com
Enchantments—www
.enchantmentsincnyc.com
HausWitch—hauswitchstore.com
Everyday Magic—
shopeverydaymagic.com
Namaste Bookshop—www
.namastebookshop.com

LEARN MORE

CRYSTALS

Energy Muse—www.energymuse.com
Goldirocks—www.goldirocks.co

ASTROLOGY

Cosmic Cousins podcast—
cosmiccousins.podbean.com

The AstroTwins—astrostyle.com
Mojave Rising—thestarparlor.com
Cafe Astrology—cafeastrology.com
Moon Club—www.moonclub.co

TAROT

Biddy Tarot—www.biddytarot.com

HERBS, TONICS & REMEDIES

Mountain Rose Herbs—www
.mountainroseherbs.com
Anima Mundi Herbals—
animamundiherbals.com
Remedies Herb Shop—
remediesherbshop.com
Lotuswei—www.lotuswei.com

SPIRITUAL WELLNESS

Mama Medicine—www
.mamamedicine.nyc
Maha Rose Center for Healing—
www.maharose.com
The Assemblage—www
.theassemblage.com/index.php

RESOURCES BY CHAPTER

INTRODUCTION

xxii **your brain processes the world:** Emmons, R. A., and McCullough, M. E. (2003). "Counting Blessings Versus Burdens: An Experimental Investigation of Gratitude and Subjective Well-Being in Daily Life." *Journal of Personality and Social Psychology* 84, no. 2: 377–89. https://greatergood.berkeley.edu/pdfs/GratitudePDFs/6Emmons-BlessingsBurdens.pdf.

xxiii **perfect illustration of the term:** Dell, C. (2016). *The Occult, Witchcraft & Magic: An Illustrated History.* London: Thames & Hudson.

INTRODUCING YOUR SPIRITUAL TOOLKIT

Crystals

2 **more than 1,500 years:** Hall, J. (2015). *Crystals: How to Use Crystals and Their Energy to Enhance Your Life.* New York: Hay House, p. 30.

2 **prevent drunkenness and hangovers:** "Amethyst." Merriam-Webster Word Central. http://unabridged.merriam-webster.com/unabridged/amethyst.

3 **what they're typically used for today:** Askinosie, H., and Jandro, T. (2017). *Crystal Muse: Everyday Rituals to Tune in to the Real You.* New York: Hay House.

4 **going for $5,000 each:** Raphael, R. (May 5, 2017). "Is There a Crystal Bubble? Inside the Billion-Dollar 'Healing' Gemstone Industry." *Fast Company.* https://www.fastcompany.com /40410406/is-there-a-crystal-bubble-inside-the-billion-dollar-healing-gemstone-industry.

Herbs and Plants

7 **"those who take care of us":** Kimmerer, R. W. (2013). *Braiding Sweetgrass: Indigenous Wisdom, Scientific Knowledge, and the Teachings of Plants.* Minneapolis, MN: Milkweed Editions.

7 **five thousand years:** de la Forêt, R. (2017). *Alchemy of Herbs: Transform Everyday Ingredients into Foods & Remedies That Heal.* New York: Hay House, p. 7.

8 **infected with the disease:** "A Brief History of Herbalism." (n.d.). University of Virginia Historical Collections at the Claude Moore Health Sciences Library. http://exhibits.hsl.virginia.edu/herbs/brief-history.

8 **around with her as proof:** Dell, *The Occult, Witchcraft & Magic*, p. 182.

Essential Oils

11 **by any other sense:** Herz, R. S. (September 2016). "The Role of Odor-Evoked Memory in Psychological and Physiological Health." *Brain Sciences* 6, no. 3. https://www.ncbi.nlm.nih.gov/pmc/articles/PMC5039451.

11 **stress and anxiety worldwide:** Williams, F. (2017*). Nature Fix: Why Nature Makes Us Happier, Healthier, and More Creative.* New York: W. W. Norton, p. 77.

12 **tapped for oil:** Worwood, V. A. (1991). *The Complete Book of Essential Oils and Aromatherapy.* Novato, CA: New World Library, p. 6.

12 **"scented massage every day":** Worwood, *The Complete Book of Essential Oils and Aromatherapy*, p. 7.

12 **upward of two hundred times:** Althea Press. (2013). *Essential Oils for Beginners: The Guide to Get Started with Essential Oils and Aromatherapy.* Berkeley, CA: Althea Press.

12 **initial journeys underground:** Grigore, A. (2017). *Just the Essentials: How Essential Oils Can Heal Your Skin, Improve Your Health, and Detox Your Life.* New York: Harper Wave, p. 14.

12 **during the bubonic plague:** Grigore, *Just the Essentials*, p. 20.

14 **"labor to describe it":** Culpeper, N. (1880). *Culpeper's Complete Herbal: Consisting of a Comprehensive Description of Nearly All Herbs with Their Medicinal Properties and Directions for Compounding the Medicines Extracted from Them.* London: Foulsham, p. 73. https://archive.org/details/culpeperscomplet00culpuoft.

14 **ones for every mood:** Althea Press, *Essential Oils for Beginners*, pp. 37–150.

15 **look into the manufacturer:** Grigore, *Just the Essentials*, p. 83.

16 **skin there is stronger:** Grigore, *Just the Essentials*, p. 11.

Astrology

19 **humans could find them:** Whitfield, P. (2004). *Astrology: A History.* London: British Library, p. 10.

19 **or animal circle:** "Zodiac (n.)." Online Etymology Dictionary. https://www.etymonline.com/word/zodiac.

19 **the cosmos could shine:** Saunders, H. (1998). "A Brief Overview of the History of Western Astrology." Astrology House. https://www.astrology-house.com/content/docs/articles/brief_history_of_western_astrology.pdf.

19 **until it reaches Paradise:** Roob, A. (2014). *Alchemy & Mysticism.* Cologne, Germany: Taschen.

19 **came in Renaissance Europe:** Saunders, "A Brief Overview of the History of Western Astrology."

19 **astrologers to plan and plot:** Whitfield, *Astrology*, p. 142.

20 in *The Sunday Express*: McRobbie, L. R. (January 5, 2016). "How Are Horoscopes Still a Thing?" Smithsonian.com. https://www.smithsonianmag.com/history/how-are-horoscopes-still-thing-180957701.

Tarot

27 **in 1909:** Hederman, M. P. (2003). *Tarot, Talisman or Taboo? Reading the World as Symbol.* Dublin: Currach Press.

Breathwork and Meditation

32 **those who only took laxatives:** Schuster, B. G. (February 2015). "Constipation in Older Adults." *Canadian Family Physician* 61, no. 2: 152–58. https://www.ncbi.nlm.nih.gov/pmc/articles/PMC4325863.

32 **bringing a sense of equilibrium:** Aust, G., and Fischer, K. (October 1997). "[Changes in Body Equilibrium Response Caused by Breathing: A Posturographic Study with Visual Feedback.]" *Laryngo-Rhino-Otologie* 76, no. 10: 577–82. https://www.ncbi.nlm.nih.gov/pubmed/9445523.

33 **"rehabilitation of criminal offenders":** Zope, S. A., and Zope, R. A. (January–June 2013). "Sudarshan Kriya Yoga: Breathing for Health." *International Journal of Yoga* 6, no. 1: 4–10. https://www.ncbi.nlm.nih.gov/pmc/articles/PMC3573542.

33 **when psychotherapy is failing:** Grof, S. (n.d.). *Holotropic Breathwork: New Perspectives in Psychotherapy and Self-Exploration.* http://wisdomuniversity.org/grof/module/week3/pdf/Holotropic%20Breathwork.pdf.

33 **an overall boost in self-awareness:** Miller, T., and Nielsen, L. (December 2015). "Measure of Significance of Holotropic Breathwork in the Development of Self-Awareness." *Journal of Alternative and Complementary Medicine* 21, no. 12: 796–803. https://www.ncbi.nlm.nih.gov/pubmed/26565611.

The Moon and the Sun

35 **unparalleled energy and force:** Choi, C. Q. (November 14, 2017). "Earth's Sun: Facts About the Sun's Age, Size and History." Space.com. https://www.space.com/58-the-sun-formation-facts-and-characteristics.html.

36 **the words "lunacy" and "lunatic":** History.com Staff. (August 27, 2013). "7 Unusual Myths and Theories About the Moon." History.com. http://www.history.com/news/history-lists/7-unusual-myths-and-theories-about-the-moon.

36 **stirring with the moon's energy:** Arkowitz, H., and Lilienfeld, S. O. (February 1, 2009). "Lunacy and the Full Moon." *Scientific American.* https://www.scientificamerican.com/article/lunacy-and-the-full-moon.

36 **increases in crime:** Arkowitz and Lilienfeld, "Lunacy and the Full Moon."

36 **greater than the sky's:** Bellebuono, H. (2012). *The Essential Herbal for Natural Health: How to Transform Easy-to-Find Herbs into Healing Remedies for the Whole Family.* Boston: Roost Books.

Crafting an Altar to Store Your Toolkit

41 **meaning "a high place":** Linn, D. (1999). *Altars: Bringing Sacred Shrines into Your Every-day Life*. New York: Ballantine.

WINTER

48 **flood of light:** Handwerk, B. (December 21, 2015). "Everything You Need to Know About the Winter Solstice." *National Geographic*. https://news.nationalgeographic.com/2015/12/151221-winter-solstice-explained-pagans.

48 **align with this event:** Handwerk, "Everything You Need to Know About the Winter Solstice."

48 **profound effects:** Haas, E. M. (2003). *Staying Healthy with the Seasons*. Berkeley, CA: Celestial Arts.

50 **the more susceptible you are:** Roecklein, K. A., and Rohan, K. J. (January 2005). "Seasonal Affective Disorder: An Overview and Update." *Psychiatry* 2, no. 1: 20–26. https://www.ncbi.nlm.nih.gov/pmc/articles/PMC3004726/.

51 **9 percent of Alaska's:** Melrose, S. (November 2015). "Seasonal Affective Disorder: An Overview of Assessment and Treatment Approaches." *Depression Research and Treatment*. https://www.hindawi.com/journals/drt/2015/178564.

59 **decisions here on Earth:** Dillon, C. R. (2001). *Superstitions and Folk Remedies*. Lincoln, NE: Authors Choice Press.

59 **bright lights of beyond:** Nozedar, A. (2008). *The Element Encyclopedia of Secret Signs and Symbols: The Ultimate A–Z Guide from Alchemy to the Zodiac*. London: Harper Element.

59 **listening to your every desire:** Nozedar, *The Element Encyclopedia of Secret Signs and Symbols*.

62 **in English alone:** "How many words are there in the English language?" *Oxford English Dictionary*. https://en.oxforddictionaries.com/explore/how-many-words-are-there-in-the-english-language

62 **cut down on our doctor visits:** Lepore, S. J. (November 1997). "Expressive Writing Moderates the Relation between Intrusive Thoughts and Depressive Symptoms." *Journal of Personality and Social Psychology* 73, no. 5: 1030–37. http://psycnet.apa.org/psycinfo/1997-43182-010.

62 **anywhere, for free:** Cameron, L. D., and Nicholls, G. (January 1998). "Expression of Stressful Experiences through Writing: Effects of a Self-Regulation Manipulation for Pessimists and Optimists." *Journal of Health Psychology* 17, no. 1: 84–92. https://www.ncbi.nlm.nih.gov/pubmed/9459075.

67 **wisdom of the other world:** Roob, *Alchemy & Mysticism*.

68 **place them on your altar:** Abrev, I. (2017). *The Little Big Book of White Spells*. Woodbury, MN: Llewellyn Publications.

70 **took on such significance:** Cohen, J. (September 13, 2012). "6 Things You May Not Know About the Gregorian Calendar." History.com. http://www.history.com/news/6-things-you-may-not-know-about-the-gregorian-calendar.

74 **inhaled through the nose:** Nautiyal, C. S., Chauhan, P. S., and Nene, Y. L. (December 2007). "Medicinal Smoke Reduces Airborne Bacteria." *Journal of Ethnopharmacology* 114, no. 3: 446–51. https://www.ncbi.nlm.nih.gov/pubmed/17913417.

74 **reduction in atmospheric bacteria:** Nautiyal, Chauhan, and Nene, "Medicinal Smoke Reduces Airborne Bacteria."

74 **lower rates of depression:** Perez, V., Alexander, D. D., and Bailey, W. H. (January 2013). "Air Ions and Mood Outcomes: A Review and Meta-Analysis." *BMC Psychiatry* 13. https://www.ncbi.nlm.nih.gov/pmc/articles/PMC3598548.

75 **dementia patients:** Tian, J., Shi, J., Zhang, X., and Wang, Y. (October 2010). "Herbal Therapy: A New Pathway for the Treatment of Alzheimer's Disease." *Alzheimer's Research & Therapy* 2, no. 30. https://alzres.biomedcentral.com/articles/10.1186/alzrt54.

79 **that deity's guidance:** Hemingway, C., and Hemingway, S. (October 2003). "Greek Gods and Religious Practices." Heilbrunn Timeline of Art History, Metropolitan Museum of Art. https://www.metmuseum.org/toah/hd/grlg/hd_grlg.htm.

79 **an existing relationship:** Cartwright, M. (June 24, 2012). "Aphrodite." Ancient History Encyclopedia. https://www.ancient.eu/Aphrodite.

79 **romantic language of flowers:** Lehner, E., and Lehner, J. (2003). *Folklore and Symbolism of Flowers, Plants and Trees: With over 200 Rare and Unusual Floral Designs and Illustrations.* Mineola, NY: Dover Publications, Inc.

79 **silently speak volumes:** Heilmeyer, M. (2008). *The Language of Flowers: Symbols and Myths.* Munich: Prestel, p. 16.

80 **the lily for peace:** Reiss, M. (2013). *Lily.* London: Reaktion Books, p. 64.

80 **passion and pain:** Heilmeyer, *The Language of Flowers*, p. 11.

82 **loving energy of its own:** Lehner and Lehner, *Folklore and Symbolism of Flowers, Plants and Trees.*

83 **extra dose of imagination:** "The History of Fairy Tales." (n.d.). Internet Sacred Text Archive. http://www.sacred-texts.com/etc/sft/sft07.htm.

83 **"poetic presentation of a spiritual truth":** Kready, L. F. (1916). *A Study of Fairy Tales.* Cambridge, MA: Riverside Press, p. 159.

83 **across time and culture:** Yong, E. (January 20, 2016). "The Fairy Tales That Predate Christianity." *The Atlantic.* https://www.theatlantic.com/science/archive/2016/01/on-the-origin-of-stories/424629.

83 ***Dance Little Baby, Dance Up High***: Cave, R., and Ayad, S. (2017). *The History of Books in 100 Books: The Complete Story, from Egypt to E-book.* Richmond Hill, ON: Firefly Books, p. 194.

SPRING

95 **most of all, roses:** Unknown Author. (1829). *The Olio, or, Museum of Entertainment*, vol. 3. London: Joseph Shackell, p. 206.

96 **fertility and harvest:** d'Aulaire, I., and d'Aulaire, E. P. (2010). *D'Aulaires' Book of Greek Myths.* New York: Scholastic.

96 **meet your mate:** Getonga, J. (2013). *European Paganism.* Muranga, Kenya: Fr. J. Getonga, p. 119.

96 **Pyramid of the Sun:** Reuters Staff. (March 21, 2016). "Mexicans Celebrate Spring Equinox at Pyramid of the Sun." Reuters. https://www.reuters.com/article/us-mexico-equinox-ruins/mexicans-celebrate-spring-equinox-at-pyramid-of-the-sun-idUSKCN0WN2CI.

102 **comes from Japan:** "Vernal Equinox Day 2018 and 2019." (n.d.). Public Holidays Global. https://publicholidays.jp/vernal-equinox-day.

107 **effect on us too:** Dunbar, B. (April 16, 2007). "Follow the Water: Finding a Perfect Match for Life." NASA Fact Sheet. https://www.nasa.gov/vision/earth/everydaylife/jamestown-water-fs.html.

111 **homage to the cycles of life:** Linn, *Altars*, pp. 58–61.

112 **where the sun rises:** Linn, *Altars*, pp. 88–93.

112 **sources of new life:** Nozedar, *The Element Encyclopedia of Secret Signs and Symbols*, pp. 51–52.

112 **the sun and the moon:** Nozedar, *The Element Encyclopedia of Secret Signs and Symbols*, pp. xiii–xiv.

115 **celebrate tea drinking:** National Tea Day. (n.d.). https://www.nationalteaday.co.uk.

115 **bringing tea to the country:** Whitehead, N. (June 30, 2015). "High Tea, Afternoon Tea, Elevenses: English Tea Times for Dummies." *The Salt*, NPR. https://www.npr.org/sections/thesalt/2015/06/30/418660351/high-tea-afternoon-tea-elevenses-english-tea-times-for-dummies.

115 **biscuits and scones:** Whitehead, "High Tea, Afternoon Tea, Elevenses."

115 **about 2700 BC:** Heiss, M. L., and Heiss, R. J. (2007). *The Story of Tea: A Cultural History and Drinking Guide*. Berkeley, CA: Ten Speed Press, p. 31.

117 **"A Highland Seer":** A Highland Seer. (1995). *Reading Tea Leaves*. New York: Clarkson Potter, pp. 62–68.

123 **"we cannot eat money":** Nelson, J. (December 19, 2011). "We Cannot Eat Money." https://www.huffingtonpost.com/jerry-nelson/we-cant-eat-money_b_1156252.html.

123 **function optimally—and we believe it:** Chevalier, G. et al. (January 2012). "Earthing: Health Implications of Reconnecting the Human Body to the Earth's Surface Electrons." *Journal of Environmental and Public Health* 2012. https://www.ncbi.nlm.nih.gov/pmc/articles/PMC3265077.

126 **been a celebration of spring:** Aveni, A. F. (2003). *The Book of the Year: A Brief History of Our Seasonal Holidays*. Oxford: Oxford University Press, pp. 79–89.

126 **Germanic Europeans in medieval times:** Getonga, *European Paganism*, p. 119.

126 **story for another day and time:** Foner, P. S. (1986). *May Day: A Short History of the International Workers' Holiday, 1886–1986*. New York: International Publishers, pp. 41–43.

128 **asymmetry and minimalism shine through:** Bugbee, S. (November 19, 2017). "Freakebana: The New, Ugly-Cool Style of Arranging Flowers." The Cut. https://www.thecut.com/2017/11/freakebana-the-new-ugly-cool-style-of-arranging-flowers.html.

130 **awareness of laughter's health benefits:** Khatchadourian, R. (August 20, 2010). "The Laughing Guru." *The New Yorker*. https://www.newyorker.com/magazine/2010/08/30/the-laughing-guru.

130 **strengthen human connections:** Savage, B. M. et al. (September 2017). "Humor, Laughter, Learning, and Health!: A Brief Review." *Advances in Physiology Education* 41, no. 3: 341–47. https://www.ncbi.nlm.nih.gov/pubmed/28679569.

130 **and stress in breast cancer patients:** Kim, S. H., Kim, Y. H., and Kim, H. J. (May 2015). "Laughter and Stress Relief in Cancer Patients: A Pilot Study." *Evidence-Based Complementary and Alternative Medicine* 2015. https://www.ncbi.nlm.nih.gov/pubmed/26064177.

130 **lower blood sugar:** Hayashi, K. et al. (May 2003). "Laughter Lowered the Increase in Postprandial Blood Glucose." *Diabetes Care* 26, no. 5: 1651–52. http://care.diabetesjournals.org/content/26/5/1651.

130 **and blood pressure:** "Humor Helps Your Heart? How?" (April 5, 2017). American Heart Association. http://www.heart.org/HEARTORG/HealthyLiving/Humor-helps-your-heart-How_UCM_447039_Article.jsp#.WhJWOLQ-fWU.

135 **before the Civil War:** History.com Staff. (n.d.). "Mother's Day." http://www.history.com/topics/holidays/mothers-day.

SUMMER

142 **splits summer into two parts:** Haas, *Staying Healthy with the Seasons.*

148 **sixteen hours as you move up to Seattle:** Grieser, J. (June 20, 2013). "The Summer Solstice: Northern Hemisphere's Longest Day, Highest Sun of the Year." *The Washington Post.* https://www.washingtonpost.com/news/capital-weather-gang/wp/2013/06/20/summer-solstice-2013-northern-hemispheres-longest-day-highest-sun-of-the-year.

148 **Artemis, the goddess of the moon:** d'Aulaire and d'Aulaire, *D'Aulaires' Book of Greek Myths.*

148 **made way for evil spirits:** Cartwright, D. (December 17, 2012). "Amaterasu." Ancient History Encyclopedia. https://www.ancient.eu/Amaterasu.

153 **(our fight-or-flight response):** Park, B. J. et al. (January 2010). "The Physiological Effects of Shinrin-yoku (Taking in the Forest Atmosphere or Forest Bathing): Evidence from Field Experiments in 24 Forests Across Japan." *Environmental Health and Preventive Medicine* 15, no. 1: 18–26. https://www.ncbi.nlm.nih.gov/pubmed/19568835.

153 **Japanese forestry ministry in 1982:** Park, B. J. et al., "The Physiological Effects of Shinrin-yoku."

154 **"Squat down and touch a plant":** Williams, *Nature Fix.*

154 **literally written in the constitution:** Helliwell, J., Layard, R., and Sachs, J. (2018). "World Happiness Report 2018." New York: Sustainable Development Solutions Network. http://worldhappiness.report/ed/2018.

154 **a rooftop garden:** Buettner, D. (November 2017). "These Are the World's Happiest Places." *National Geographic.* https://www.nationalgeographic.com/magazine/2017/11/worlds-happiest-places.

157 *The Twelve Healers and Other Remedies:* Bach, E. (1997). *The Twelve Healers and Other Remedies.* Saffron Walden, England: C. W. Daniel.

157 **prone to high blood pressure:** Moyer, A. E. et al. (May 1994). "Stress-Induced Cortisol Response and Fat Distribution in Women." *Obesity Research* 2, no. 3: 255–62. https://www.ncbi.nlm.nih.gov/pubmed/16353426.

157 **and heart disease:** Whitworth, J. A. et al. (December 2005). "Cardiovascular Consequences of Cortisol Excess." *Vascular Health and Risk Management* 1, no. 4: 291–99. https://www.ncbi.nlm.nih.gov/pmc/articles/PMC1993964.

161 **kissing played a romantic role:** Jankowiak, W. R., Volsche, S. L., and Garcia, J. R. (September 2015). "Is the Romantic–Sexual Kiss a Near Human Universal?" *American Anthropologist* 117, no. 3: 535–39. http://onlinelibrary.wiley.com/doi/10.1111/aman.12286/full#aman12286-sec-0050.

162 **a kissable person makes for a good mate:** "The 'Science of Kissing.'" (February 11, 2011). NPR. https://www.npr.org/2011/02/11/133686008/The-Science-Of-Kissing.

162 **the "stress" hormone, in both partners:** Associated Press. "Mwah! Kissing Eases Stress, Study Finds." (February 13, 2009). NBCNews.com. http://www.nbcnews.com/id/29187964/ns/health-behavior/t/mwah-kissing-eases-stress-study-finds.

166 **on the light they're exposed to:** Gonzalez, R. (March 6, 2015). "10 Gemstones Much Rarer Than Diamond." Gizmodo. https://io9.gizmodo.com/5902212/ten-gemstones-that-are-rarer-than-diamond.

167 **recognized by the United Nations:** "International Day of Friendship." (n.d.). United Nations. http://www.un.org/en/events/friendshipday.

167 **makes us less self-conscious as adults:** Bagwell, C. L., Newcomb, A. F., and Bukowski, W. M. (February 1998). "Preadolescent Friendship and Peer Rejection as Predictors of

Adult Adjustment." *Child Development* 69, no. 1: 140–53. https://www.ncbi.nlm.nih.gov /pubmed/9499563.

167 **negative interactions with immediate family members:** Rubin, K. H. et al. (November 2004). "Attachment, Friendship, and Psychosocial Functioning in Early Adolescence." *Journal of Early Adolescence* 24, no. 4: 326–56. https://www.ncbi.nlm.nih.gov/pubmed /16703116.

167 **hugs can actually reduce stress:** Rea, S. (December 17, 2014). "Hugs Help Protect Against Stress and Infection, Say Carnegie Mellon Researchers." Carnegie Mellon University. https://www.cmu.edu/news/stories/archives/2014/december/december17_hugsprotect .html.

167 **the pressure of social media:** Singal, J. (March 13, 2016). "For 80 Years, Young Americans Have Been Getting More Anxious and Depressed." The Cut. https://www.thecut .com/2016/03/for-80-years-young-americans-have-been-getting-more-anxious-and -depressed.html.

173 **weaver girl in Chinese mythology:** Huang, E. (August 25, 2017). "The Story of Chinese Valentine's Day Teaches Us True Love Is Worth Waiting For." Quartz. https://qz.com /1062110/chinese-valentines-day-what-is-the-story-behind-qi-xi-%E4%B8%83%E5%A4 %95-and-how-is-it-celebrated.

177 **followed the dead into their tombs:** Cave and Ayad, *The History of Books in 100 Books.*

177 **constructed the Library of Alexandria to house them:** El-Abbadi, M. (May 12, 2016). "Library of Alexandria." *Encyclopaedia Britannica.* https://www.britannica.com/topic /Library-of-Alexandria.

177 **collect all the knowledge of mankind:** Cave and Ayad, *The History of Books in 100 Books*, p. 37.

182 **when critters chomp at their leaves:** Haskell, D. G. (2017). *The Songs of Trees: Stories from Nature's Great Connectors.* New York: Viking, p. 37.

182 **fungi buried beneath the soil:** Toomey, D. (September 1, 2016). "Exploring How and Why Trees 'Talk' to Each Other." Yale Environment 360. https://e360.yale.edu/features /exploring_how_and_why_trees_talk_to_each_other.

182 **infinite biological pathways below the ground:** Simard, S. (June 2016). "How Trees Talk to Each Other." TEDSummit. https://www.ted.com/talks/suzanne_simard_how _trees_talk_to_each_other.

183 **all come with stories attached:** Kinver, M. (April 5, 2017). "World Is Home to '60,000 Tree Species.'" BBC. http://www.bbc.com/news/science-environment-39492977.

183 **a symbol of freedom and perseverance:** Newman, C. (March 2017). "What We Can Learn from Trees." *National Geographic.* https://www.nationalgeographic.com/maga zine/2017/03/wisdom-of-trees.

183 **claim to have heard the trees sing:** Haskell, *The Songs of Trees*, p. 15.

AUTUMN

188 **and eating moon cakes:** Custer, C. (March 6, 2017). "All About the Chinese Moon Festival." ThoughtCo. https://www.thoughtco.com/profile-of-the-chinese-moon-festival-4077070.

188 **corn and other grains wilted and died:** "The Interworking of the Three Sisters" (n.d.). http://www.oneidaindiannation.com/the-interworking-of-the-three-sisters/

189 **is the aurora borealis:** Rao, J. (September 20, 2012). "Fall Equinox Saturday Ups Chances of Seeing Northern Lights." Space.com. https://www.space.com/17692-fall-equinox -northern-lights.html.

205 **whichever is closer to the autumnal equinox:** Schaaf, F. (n.d.). "What Is a Harvest Moon?" Old Farmer's Almanac. https://www.almanac.com/content/what-harvest-moon.

205 **creates a shallow angle at dusk:** Crockett, C. (January 2017). "Ecliptic Traces the Sun's Path." EarthSky. http://earthsky.org/astronomy-essentials/what-is-the-ecliptic.

206 **stroke and cancer patients to heal faster:** Merz, B. (November 5, 2015). "Healing Through Music." Harvard Health Blog. https://www.health.harvard.edu/blog/healing -through-music-201511058556.

206 **placebo-controlled counterparts:** Kearl, A. (2017). "The Swiss Resonance Monochord Table: Inquiry into the Healing Complexity and Transformative Power of Sound." San Francisco, CA: California Institute of Integral Studies. https://www.tandfonline.com /doi/abs/10.1300/J094v05n03_04.

206 **patients who didn't receive vibrations:** Butler C., Butler P. (1997). "Physioacoustic Therapy with Cardiac Surgery Patients." In Wigram, T., and Dileo, C., eds. *Music Vibration and Health*. Cherry Hill, NJ: Jeffrey Books, pp. 197–204.

206 **more than when we sing together:** Schäfer, T. et al. (August 2013). "The Psychological Functions of Music Listening." *Frontiers in Psychology* 4, no. 511. https://www.ncbi.nlm .nih.gov/pmc/articles/PMC3741536.

206 **potency and potential to soothe:** Schäfer, "The Psychological Functions of Music Listening."

206 **in fact creative energy manifested:** Mahdihassan, S. (January and April 1989). "The Symbols of Creative Energy in the Literature on Mysticism and on Alchemy." *Ancient Science of Live* VIII, nos. 3–4: 191–95.

210 **as powerful as medication in some cases:** Park, S. H., and Han, K. S. (September 2017). "Blood Pressure Response to Meditation and Yoga: A Systematic Review and Meta-Analysis." *Journal of Alternative and Complementary Medicine* 23, no. 9: 685–95. https:// www.ncbi.nlm.nih.gov/pubmed/28384004.

211 **universal, languageless sound:** Levine, M. (July 14, 2011). "5 Facts You May Not Know About 'OM.'" mindbodygreen. https://www.mindbodygreen.com/0-2776/5-Facts-You -May-Not-Know-About-OM.html.

211 **stems from Kundalini yoga:** Kaur, R. (Mary 30, 2012). "Sat Nam: The Kundalini Mantra of Awareness." Spirit Voyage. http://www.spiritvoyage.com/blog/index.php/sat-nam -the-kundalini-mantra-of-awareness.

216 **winter and the end of the harvest season:** History.com Staff. (2009). "Halloween 2018." History.com. http://www.history.com/topics/halloween/history-of-halloween.

217 **considered the oldest form of magic:** Dell, *The Occult, Witchcraft & Magic*, p. 112.

222 **on other Fridays in November:** Hesse, M. (November 11, 2011). "11/11/11 Is a Divine Date for Many Interested in Numbers." *The Washington Post*. https://www.washington post.com/lifestyle/style/111111-is-a-divine-date-for-many-interested-in-numbers/2011 /11/08/gIQA1S7p9M_story.html.

225 **"all of Japanese society":** Wastler, A. (November 13, 2017). "Living Mutual: Creating Kindness Day." MassMutual. https://blog.massmutual.com/post/kindness-day

226 **happier and more satisfied with their lives:** Buchanan, K. E., and Bardi, A. (August 2010). "Acts of Kindness and Acts of Novelty Affect Life Satisfaction." *Journal of Social Psychology* 150, no. 3: 235–37. http://www.tandfonline.com/doi/abs/10.1080/0022454090 3365554.

229 **culture, religion, or group of people:** History.com Staff. (2009). "Thanksgiving 2018." History.com http://www.history.com/topics/thanksgiving/history-of-thanksgiving.

231 **leading hospitals throughout the country:** Green Lotus. (2011). "Reiki Really Works: A Groundbreaking Scientific Study." Green Lotus. https://www.uclahealth.org/rehab /workfiles/Urban%20Zen/Research%20Articles/Reiki_Really_Works-A_Groundbreak ing_Scientific_Study.pdf.

235 **magic and sorcery through words:** Dell, *The Occult, Witchcraft & Magic*, p. 22.

235 **finding love, gaining power, and treating disease:** Choat, M., and Gardner, I. (2013). *A Coptic Handbook of Ritual Power*. Turnhout, Belgium: Brepols.

235 **words and names hold mystical force:** Dell, *The Occult, Witchcraft & Magic*, pp. 41–72.

235 **"impotent without words":** De Laurence, L. W. (1915, 2007). *Great Book of Magical Art, Hindu Magic and East Indian Occultism, and the Book of Secret Hindu, Ceremonial, and Talismanic Magic*. Digireads, p. 103.

INDEX

Page numbers in *italics* indicate illustrations.

downward-facing dog pose, 170
Drawing Ritual for Magnificence, 148–52, *149*
Drawing Ritual for Rebirth, 85–87
Drop into the Presence spread, 180–81
Duanwu (Dragon Boat) Festival, 143
Dust II Onyx deck, 28

Earth Day, 122–25
Earth signs, 21, *23*, 23–24, *24*, 26, 72, 73
Easter, 97–98, 102
eclipses, 38, 205
ego, xxii, 49, 70, 208, 237
Egyptians, 2, 12, 48, 98, 177, 229, 235
80/20 approach, xvi, 2
11/11 (November 11), 222–24
Elevenses (teatime), 115
emerald, *3*, 4
emotional support, crystals for, 164
Empowerment, Affirmation Ritual for, 213–15
Encouragement, Astrology Ritual for, 70–73
Enduring Love, Sound Healing Ritual for,
     xvii, 174–76
energy, xxii, 2, 3, 4, 5, 8, 9, 21, 22, 23, 24, 25,
     27, 28, 30, 33, 35, 36, 38, 39, 40
     See also specific energies
Energy, Aromatherapy Ritual for, 17
Energy, Botanical Arrangement Ritual for,
     127–29
energy, essential oils for, 14
England, 55, 59, 80, 115, 229
equinox, 39, 95
essential oils, 9, 11–17, *13*, 44, 67, 68, 80, 81,
     87, 102, 104, 105, 110, 114
Europe, 12, 19, 80, 89, 126, 142, 177, 183, 225
Expansion, Flower Essence Ritual for, 159–60
Exploration, Forest Bath Ritual for, 154–56, *155*
Expression, Astro Reading Ritual for, 27

facial steam, 10, 80–82, *82*
fairy tale day, 83–87, *84*
Faith, Planting Ritual for, 56–58
fall. *See* autumn
fall violet blossom honey, 121
family and new beginnings *gua*, *76*, 77
Femininity, Floral Facial Steam for, 10,
     80–82, *82*
feng shui, *76*, 76–77

fertility awareness method, 137–39, *138*
figure-eight and healing, 75–76
Fire Ritual for Release, 40–41
fire signs, 23, *23*, 24, *24*, 26, 72, 73
first full moon of
     autumn, *204*, 205–9
     spring, 111–14
     summer, 157–60, *158*
     winter, 62–64
     See also full moons
first new moon of
     autumn, 199–203
     spring, *107*, 107–10
     summer, 153–56, *155*
     winter, 59–61, *61*
     See also new moons
fixed signs, 73
Floral Facial Steam for Femininity and
     Self-Love, 10, 80–82, *82*
Flower Essence Ritual for Expansion, 159–60
flower essences, 82, 128–29, 157
flower power, 79–80, 159
focus, essential oils for, 14
Forest Bathing Ritual for Exploration,
     154–56, *155*
Frank, Anne, 183
frankincense, 12, 14
Free-Form Drawing Ritual for Magnificence,
     148–52, *149*
Fresh Start, Smudging for, 10
Freud, Sigmund, xxii
Friday the 13th, 224
friendship, 143, 167–72, *169*
full moons, 27, 36, 37, *37*, 38, 39, 40, 93, 107,
     111, 113, 143, 188, 205, 206
     See also first full moon; moon and the sun

garlic, 194
Gemini, *20*, 23, *23*, 26, 40, 72, 73
Gestalt psychology, 168, 196
Giri, Ananda, 174
going full circle, *216*, 216–17
Golden Thread Tarot app, 179
Good Luck, Talisman Crafting Ritual for,
     222–24
good vibrations, 205–6
Google, 15–16, 64, 66

gratitude, xxii, 49, 91, 124, 135, 154, 185, 188

Greeks, 2–3, 12, 19, 70, 79, 96, 122, 148, 177, 188, 229

green crystals, 165

Green Gold (nettle) Infusion, 118–20

Gregory XIII (Pope), 70

Grof, Stan, 33

grounding, 196–98

Grounding, Crystal Ritual for, 123–25

Grounding, Reiki-Inspired Ritual for Healing, 230, 231–34

Growth, Moonlit Yoga Ritual for, 108–10

gua sha, 105–6

Guidance, Mandala Ritual for, 217–21

Gutenberg, Johann, 177

Hades, 96, 188

Hailes, Natalia, 137–39

Halloween, 190, 216, 216–21

Hanukkah, 49, 66

harvest moon, 205–6

Harvest Ritual for Abundance, 195–98

Healing, Grounding Reiki Ritual for, 230, 231–34

Health, Blended Balm Ritual for Good, 17

health gua, 76, 77

hearing (sense), 86

heating breath (bhastrika), 34

hematite, 2–3, 165

Henry VII (King of England), 19

herbs and plants, 7–11, 55–58

Hercules, 19

hero's pose, 108, 109

Hess, Katie, 160

"Highland Seer, A," 117

Hindus, 210

Hippocrates, 12

"holding space," xxii–xxiii, 39, 88, 90, 92, 137

holidays and rituals, xx
    See also specific holidays

holotropic breathwork, 33

Home Ritual for Clarity, 75–77, 76

honeybees, 142

horoscopes, 18, 19–21

houses and astrology, 22, 73

hugs and immune system, 167

Humming Ritual, Tuning In, 114, 205–6, 206–9

ikebana, 128

Incense Ritual for Deep Work, 11

India, 2, 8, 210, 225

Insight, Tassology Ritual for, 116, 116–18

Instagram, 212, 213

intention, xxiii, 2, 5, 6, 41
    See also specific rituals

Intention, Journaling Ritual for, 62–64

International Day of Friendship, 143, 167–72

International Day of Peace, 182–85

International Kissing Day, 143, 161–62

International Women's Day, 88–93

International Workers' Day, 126

intuition, xxiii, 4, 6, 27, 28, 29, 30
    See also specific rituals

Ise Grand Shrine, 148

Japan, 102, 115, 128, 148, 153–54, 188, 225, 235

Jarvis, Ann Reeves, 135

jasmine, 12, 13, 14, 55, 160

Jesus, 97–98

Jews, 97–98

Joan of Arc, 8

journaling, 124, 235, 235–38

Journaling Ritual for Intention, 62–64

Journaling Ritual for Self-Reflection, 31

kapalabhati (energizing breath), 33, 199–202

karmic debt number, 224

Kataria, Dr. Madan, 130

Katonah yoga, 108, 168

Kaya, Seiji, 225

Keates, Dages Juvelier, 116, 118–21

Kellner, Lindsay, xi–xiii, 26, 32, 108, 211–13, 237, 239
    See also Spirit Almanac

kindness, 225–28

Kirshenbaum, Sheril, 162

kissing, 143, 161–62

knowledge and self-cultivation gua, 76, 77

kotodama, 235

Kuhn, Natalie, 227–28

Kundalini yoga, 32, 201, 211

Kwanzaa, 49, 66

laughter, 130–34, *131,* 167
lavender, 9, *13,* 14, 15, 75, 80, 102, 104, 114
Leaves of Change, 117–18
left side stretch, 109
legs up the wall, 134
lemon, *13,* 14, 17, 110
Leo, 19, *20,* 22, 23, *23,* 26, 40, 72, 73, 88–89
Letter Writing Day, *235,* 235–38
Libra, *20,* 24, *24,* 40, 72, 73
libraries, 177
Library of Alexandria, 177
life transitions, crystals for, 165
Lincoln, Abraham, 229
linden trees, 183
lips and kissing, 161–62
listening techniques, 92, 208–9
Loewe, Emma, xi–xiii, 17, 26, 30, 34–35, 65–66, 73, 88–89, 239
  See also Spirit Almanac
love, 79–80, 174–76
loving Mother Earth, 122–23
Luna, 36
lunar holidays, 38–39
lymphatic drainage massage, 105–6

Mack, Lindsay, 180–81
magic, xvi, xx, xxiii, xxiv, 29, 35, 39, 45
  See also specific rituals
Magnificence, Free-Form Drawing Ritual for, 148–52, *149*
Major Arcana cards, 27
Make a Difference Day, *210,* 210–15
making the sky work for you, *37,* 37–39
Makrasana (crocodile pose), 132–33
Mallis, Paula, 91–93
Mandala Ritual for Guidance, 217–21
manifestation, xxiii–xxiv, 22, 38, 39, 41, 43
  See also specific rituals
Manifestation, Placement Ritual for, 111–14
mantras, *210,* 210–13
Margaret, Princess, 20
marriage *gua, 76,* 77
matcha tea, 115
May Day, *126,* 126–29
maypole ceremony, 126, 141–42
medicine wheels, 111–14

meditation, xi, xxii, 5, 44, 49, 76, 113–14, 174–75, 185, 188, 197–98, 210–11, 212, 213, 215, 239
  See also breathwork
memory and herbs, 74–75
Mercury, 21
meteorites, 4
Methuselah tree, Inyo National Forest, 182
metta meditation, 174–75
Michaan, Nevine, 108, 168
midheaven, 72
Midsummer Night's Dream, A (Shakespeare), 142
Mildon, Emma, 164–65
Milky Way, 59, 173
mindfulness meditation, 32, 215
Minimalist Oracle deck, 28
Minor Arcana cards, 27
modern autumn ritual, 189–93
modern spring ritual, 97–101
modern summer ritual, 143–47
modern winter ritual, 49–54
moon and the sun, 34–41, *37*
  See also full moons; new moons
moon circles, xvii, 39
Moon Club, 88
Moonlit Yoga Ritual for Growth, 108–10
moon signs, 21, 22, 26, 27, 71, 72
Morgan-Greer deck, 28
morning pages (*Artist's Way*), 237–38
Mother Earth, 122–23
Mother's Day, 135–39
Mount Kilimanjaro, 166
Muir, John, 153
multi-card tarot card spread, 30, 178–81
mutable signs, 73

Narine, Ramesh Tarun, 132–34
NASA, 55, 107
natal charts, 18, 21–22, 25, 71–73
National Tea Day, 115–21, *116*
Native Americans, 59, 122–23, 124, 141, 188, 229
Natural Resources Defense Council, 124
Nature Conservancy, 124
nature's rhythms, xiii, xvi, xix, xx, xxiv, 36, 47, 111, 122–23, 187

Naylor, R. H., 19–21
Nebuchadnezzar II (Babylonian king), 55
Neese, Ashley, 202–3
negative energy, xxii, 40, 74, 163
negative self-talk, 227–28
nettles, 97, 118–20
new moons, 36, *37*, 37–38, 39–40, 49, 60,
    88–89, 93, 107, 200
    See also first new moon; moon and the sun
Newton, Sir Isaac, 183
New Year's Day, 49, 74–77, *76*
New Year's Eve, 49, 70–73
north node and astrology, 21, 22
Nowruz, 95–96
numerology, 222

Ohigan, 188
Old Tjikko, 182
oleation, 97
Olympic Games, 142
om (mantra), 210, 211
One, the, 220
"Oneness Om, The" (Giri), 174
one on one, 222
1:1 and 1:2 Breathing, 133–34, 156
onyx, 165, 217
Open Heart, Crystal Ritual for, 162–66
oracle decks, 28, 30
orange crystals, 165

palo santo, 91, 108, 110, 114, 162, 163, 164,
    174, 231, 232
parasympathetic nerve activity, 153
Partner Ritual for Stability, 89–93
Partner Yoga Ritual for Unity, 168–72, *169*
Passover, 97–98, 102
Patel, Kelsey, 231, 233–34
peace, 182–85
perfectionism, 63, 218, 227, 237
Persephone, 96, 188
Persia, 48, 95–96
pheromones, 162
picnics, 142
Pictorial Key to the Tarot, The (Waite), 27
Pisces, *20*, 25, *25*, 40, 72, 73
Placement Ritual for Manifestation, 111–14
planets and astrology, 21, 22, 72

plank pose, 170
Planting Ritual for Faith, 56–58
plants, 7–11, 55–58
Plug, Britta, 105–6
Pluto, 21
Poseidon, 79
positive energy, xxii, 8, 9, 76
pranayama/pranayam, 31, 32
Presence, Writing Ritual for, 236–38
Presence Spread, Drop into the, 180–81
present-giving ritual, starting, 185
present-moment awareness, 210
psychics, 65–66
pulling a tarot card, 28–30
Pythagoras, 19

qi, 77
Qi Xi Festival, 173–76
qua, 76, *76,* 77
quartz, 2, *3,* 4, 217

Racioppi, Jennifer, 72–73
Radiance, Stargazing Ritual for, 60–61, *61*
rapid-fire rituals. *See specific rituals*
Reading Tea Leaves ("A Highland Seer"), 117
Rebirth, Drawing Ritual for, 85–87
recognition and fame *gua,* *76,* 77
red crystals, 165
Reflection Ritual for Self-Love, 226–28
Reiki, *230,* 231–34
Release, Diaphragmatic Breath, 130–34, *131*
Release, Fire Ritual for, 40–41
Renaissance, 19, 27
resolutions, 49, 70
respiratory system, 189
Reykjavik, 148
Richardson, Tanya Carroll, 69
Rider-Waite tarot deck, 27–28
right side stretch, 109
rising (ascendant) signs, 21, 22, 26, 71, 72
rituals, xi–xii, xvii–xviii, xx–xxi, xxii, xxiii,
    xxiv, 44, 239
    See also specific rituals
Romans, 36, 148, 229
Rooting Ritual for Solidarity, 183–85
Roots to Rise Infusion, 120
rosemary, *13,* 14, 80, 81

Rosenthal, Norman, 50
rose quartz, 3, *3*, 77, 164
roses, 12, 80, 82, 95
Roxo, Alexandra, 88
ruling planet, 21, 72

sage, 8, 28, 44, 75, 91, 110, 179
sage sticks, 5, 9, 28
Sagittarius, *20*, 24, *24*, 40, 72, 73
salt, 8
Salt Bath Ritual for Cleansing, 102–6, *103*
Samhain, 190, *216*, 216–21
sandalwood, 12, 14, 114
Sanskrit, 168, 188, 211, 215, 217
Satch, Christopher, 57–58
sat nam (mantra) 210, 211
Saturn, 21
savasana pose, 171, 172
Sawyers, Kumi, 109–10
Scandinavia, 48, 141–42
scent, 11, 74–75
Science of Kissing, The (Kirshenbaum), 162
Scorpio, *20*, 24, *24*, 26, 40, 72, 73
Seamless Transition, Tarot Ritual for, *178*, 178–81
seasonal affective disorder (SAD), 50–51
seasons, xviii, xix, xx, xxi, 6, 16, 22
    See also specific seasons
seed pose, 109
self-awareness, xvi
self-care, xvii
Self-Love, Floral Facial Steam for, 10, 80–82, *82*
Self-Love, Reflection Ritual for, 226–28
Self-Reflection, Journaling Ritual for, 31
Selhub, Eva, 51
semantic satiation/saturation, 211
Seventh Evening Festival, 173–76
Shakespeare, William, 142
shamans, 7, 19, 74
shanti (mantra), 210, 211
Shennong Ben Cao Jing (The Classic of Herbal Medicine), 7–8
shinrin-yoku, 153–54
Shinto religion, 148
shooting stars, 59
Shunbun no Hi, 102, 188

Sierra Club, 124
sight (sense), 86
Single-Card Pull for Support, 30
sisterhood, song of, 88–89
sitali (cooling breath), 33–34
sleep, essential oils for, 14
smell (sense), 87
Smith, Pamela Colman, 27
smudging, 9, 10, 28, 74–75
soham (mantra), 210, 211
Solidarity, Rooting Ritual for, 183–85
solo artist date weekly, 238
solstice, 39
song of sisterhood, 88–89
Sosigenes, 70
souls, interaction of our, xvi
Soul Spread, Check-in for, 180
sound baths, xvii, 174–76
Sound Healing Ritual for Enduring Love, xvii, 174–76
sounds, healing power of, 205–9
south node and astrology, 21
special lunar holidays, 38–39
spirit, xv–xvi, xvii, xxii
spirit guides, 65, 68, 69, 219–21, 222
spirit toolkit, xv–xvi, 1–45, *42*
spirituality, xxiv, 22, 77, 81, 165
Spivak, Ashley, 137–39
spring, xviii, xix, xxi, 23, 47, 70, *94*, 95–139, 144, 188, 189, 194
Squanto, 229
Stability, Partner Ritual for, 89–93
standing mountain poses, 170, 172
Stargazing Ritual for Radiance, 60–61, *61*
stargazing, 59–61
Strabo, Walahfrid, 79–80
Sudarshan Kriya yoga, 32–33
Sumerians, 62, 235
summer, xviii, xix, xxi, 23–24, 48, *140*, 141–85, 187, 190, 194
sunflowers, 80, 82
sun signs, 18, 21, 22, 26, 71, 72, 73
supermoon, 38
Support, Single-Card Pull for, 30
Sweden, 148, 154, 182
sweet basil, *13*, 14
sympathetic activity, 153

ABOUT THE AUTHORS

EMMA LOEWE is a NYC-based writer and editor. She is currently the sustainability editor at mindbodygreen, where she also covers home and spirituality content. She graduated from Duke University with a degree in environmental science in 2015 and is fascinated by how people interact with nature. She loves being outside, taking photos, and finding creative ways to write about sustainability.

LINDSAY KELLNER is currently the senior beauty and lifestyle editor at mindbodygreen, where she reports on wellness trends, mental health, inner beauty, and everything in between. She also has her own blog and podcast, Well Aware, through which she explores the intersection of spirituality and creativity with her guests and listeners. Lindsay is a 200-hour certified yoga teacher and practices at Sky Ting in New York City. She has a degree in journalism and psychology from New York University. When she's not writing, she enjoys figure drawing and painting. She lives in Brooklyn with her husband and cat.